WARWICK TODD
Goes the Tonk

WARWICK TODD
Goes the Tonk

Australia's Cricket Legend
Hits Out Again

Without a foreword by Richie Benaud

AS TOLD TO TOM GLEISNER

ABC
BOOKS

Published by ABC Books for the
AUSTRALIAN BROADCASTING CORPORATION
GPO Box 9994 Sydney NSW 2001

Copyright © Tom Gleisner 2001

First published November 2001

National Library of Australia
Cataloguing-in-Publication entry

Gleisner, Tom, 1962 – .
Warwick Todd goes the tonk.

ISBN 0 7333 1024 9.

1. Cricket – Humor. I. Australian Broadcasting
Corporation. II. Title.

641.5994

Designed and typeset by
Deborah Brash/Brash Design Pty Ltd
Cover design by Robert Taylor
Photo manipulations by Robert Taylor
Set in 9.5/15pt Stone Informal
Colour separations by Pageset, Victoria
Printed and bound in Australia by Shannon Books, Victoria

2 4 5 3 1

Acknowledgments

As always I am extremely grateful to a number of people who helped in the production of this book. Others, however, deserve a right kick up the arse. That chick who answers the phone at ABC Publishing for example. I haven't given my all on the cricket field for the best part of two decades just to have some seventeen year old with a ring through her nose put me on hold for half an hour only to then claim 'I'm sorry, he's in a meeting' every time you ring up to track down an overdue royalty cheque which, I might add, is still to arrive.

Sincere thanks must however go to my editor Stuart Neal, and of course the chick who did design. I forget her name but she knows who she is and that's the main thing. Finally, a big pat on the back for my sister-in-law Beverley who helped out with the prove-reading.

I would also like to thank my old mate Deano for agreeing to write the Foreword at such short notice. Obviously none of us expected a professional like Richie Benaud to pull out at the very last minute in quite the manner he did, having made a firm commitment to both me and the publishers which, as a former captain and respected media figure, you'd think could be fairly comfortably relied upon, but that's life I guess. No point dwelling on it. If a former Aussie skipper who, let's be frank, has done pretty well from the game, can't find the time to cobble a few paragraphs together to help out a fellow Test legend then so be it. End of story. Time to move on. Still, it's little wonder people are losing interest in the sport.

Finally, a word of thanks to my erstwhile stats man and researcher Bill Pinnell who spent a considerable amount of time and care compiling an extensive record of my Test and one-day career over the past year. It undoubtedly took a big effort from Billy and I'm just sorry we decided to drop that section.

Will this do? I've bullshitted a bit
about the batting and got rid of
all those references to Tony Grieg
and the you-know-what.
Would have written more but I've promised
Tubby an introduction and Dougie Walters
wants help with another book of humorous
anecdotes.

P.S. Could you make the cheque out
to "cash"?

Cheers   Deano

Foreword

It seems like only yesterday that Toddy made his Test debut for Australia. From memory he didn't exactly set the cricketing world on fire, returning figures of just 47, 22 and a $3000 match fine for umpire abuse, but it was the promise of things to come.

We first met in 1987 when Toddy was selected as part of the Ashes squad touring England. He became a popular and well-liked member of the team from day one. By day three he was starting to give us all the shits but that's just typical of the man.

Warwick Todd has always been a competitor who never gave anything less than everything he had and sometimes even more, depending on the batting conditions. No matter how tough the tour or how desperate the situation Toddy could always be relied upon to produce 110 per cent. Once, during a three-day tour match at Edgbaston he is reported to have given 114 per cent but that figure remains unconfirmed.

He's a man who, over the years, has worn many hats: cricketer, tourist, author, journeyman, husband, father, litigant — but whatever the label, Toddy's worn it with pride. A tough team-man, he's the sort of bloke who'll always back himself to win, often at quite attractive odds. Like all Aussies he hates to lose and his fierce, competitive streak never fades, regardless of whether he's facing an Allan Donald thunderbolt or a twelve-year-old fan with an autograph book.

In closing, I'm reminded of a story from 1989. It was the third Test against the West Indies at the MCG and we were copping some fierce bowling from the likes of Patrick Patterson and Malcolm Marshall. I suffered a cracked rib early in the innings but went on to graft 18 tough runs on a completely unpredictable pitch, including the only boundary scored in front of the wicket that day. This incident doesn't relate all that directly to Toddy — in fact, he wasn't even playing — but I was told he wanted an anecdote and that's the only one I could think of.

Good on ya mate.

Deano

Dedication

To my wife Ros.
As we float together on
the sea of married life,
she has always been
my rock.

And to all the cricketers around the world
I have ever played with or against.
No matter how fierce our battles may have
been I maintain the deepest respect
for every one of them.*

*Except Arjuna Ranatunga,
who I've hated since the day we first met.

Introduction

To tell the truth, this book almost never got written. Following the enormous impact of my last diary (no literary awards but at the time of writing there are still seven separate legal actions pending) it was decided by the 'experts' at ABC Publishing that I would be better off working with a co-writer. 'Someone to simply keep things on track' was the precise wording. This brilliant idea lasted about two days. What happened was, they sent some university-educated wanker round to sit with me and record my memories of each day's play. Torsten (believe it or not that was his name) would then go off and 're-work' my match report and anecdotes into a completely unrecognisable form. Here's an example of how it would work . . .

Day 27 by W Todd

It was another hot day in Bombay when Tugga won the toss and sent the home team into bat. Hados got off to a great start, really middling the ball and working the singles. With the field slowly pushed back, by the luncheon interval we were well placed at 1 for 134.

That was as I recalled it. Straight, simple, down-the-line and, I think you'll agree, pretty compelling. Not according to Torsten, who decided to 'spruce' things up a little. Take a squizz at what he sent back . . .

Day 27

As the dazzling orb of a subcontinental sun broke through the Mumbai haze in much the way a headlight beam penetrates a dense fog, Matthew Lawrence Hayden strode ebulliently to the crease, his first resounding stroke summoning to mind Goethe's declaration that 'boldness brings mighty forces to its aid'.

Who the f**k did Goethe play for? Anyway, the creative relationship ended there, with me giving Torsten an almighty kick up the arse (a physical act I suspect he enjoyed a little too much) and yours truly telling ABC Books that it's either me solo or you can put out another biography of Alan McGilvray. I think they saw the light and the result is the diary you're about to read . . .

FINE PINE FURNITURE

February 2001

By the end of the summer season Australian cricket had never looked so healthy. After a record number of Test and one-day wins on the trot, comparisons were even being made between us and the legendary 'Invincibles' team of 1948–49. Speaking modestly I'd have to say most of us blokes in the team found such comparisons a little embarrassing, as we were clearly a superior team. But with so much on-field success competition within the team for a berth on the upcoming tour of India was pretty intense. As a batsman I knew there were at least six other blokes putting their hand up for my spot and that selection in the subcontinent squad could not ever be taken for granted. I realised that for me, Warwick Todd, to make the side I would have to:

1 Get fit
2 Make plenty of runs at state level
3 Offer to pay for the damage to Trevor Hohns's car.

Working against me was the fact I'd missed quite a bit of play over the summer due to a recurring knee problem. I had an operation on it last October and spent two months with my left leg in plaster recuperating at home. Some people might think that sounds like fun but I can tell you it sure is not, sitting round all day with nothing to do but eat and drink. It's sort of like an extended Ashes tour only you don't get to play golf.

Having toured India before I was well aware of the special demands placed on cricketers over there and I spent a fair bit of time working out in a special acclimatisation chamber designed to replicate the hot and humid conditions of the subcontinent. It wasn't technically a 'chamber', more the front bar of Brisbane's Kent Hotel, but with the air-conditioner switched off and a few dozen mates packed in on a Friday night you could get a real feel for challenges ahead. I spent a lot of time in there acclimatising, sometimes staggering home acclimatised out of my head.

Acclimatising to the hot and humid conditions of the subcontinent.

Test cricketer fails test

By **DAVID ZINGER**

Controversial Test cricketer Warwick Todd made a brief appearance at Brisbane's Magistrates Court yesterday where he was fined $2000 and had his licence cancelled for a year after blowing .19 in a police road-side breath test. Appearing for himself, Todd told Magistrate Jeff Hume that he'd simply had "one for the road". Further questioning revealed this "one" was in fact a slab. Before passing sentence the court heard of Todd's extensive work with charity and his promise to attend alcohol management classes in the near future.

Despite all the hard work in late January I got the phone call I was dreading, telling me that I was 'out'. It was only when I heard laughing in the background that I realised it was just Slats making another of his prank calls. I guess this was a payback for my prank call to him a few years back when I'd phoned the church on the morning of his wedding to say there was a bomb under the altar. Everything ended well (for me that is, the wedding had to be cancelled) because a few hours later I got a real call from the selectors. Warwick Todd was off to India.

Tuesday February 13

Depart Sydney for Mumbai, via Hong Kong

I tell you what, after ten years on the international cricket circuit leaving home never gets any easier. Those last goodbyes can be pretty emotional and I'm not ashamed to admit there was a tear in the old Todd eye as I scrawled a hurried 'See you in April' onto a Post-It note and stuck it to the fridge.

The scene at Sydney airport was surprisingly subdued. I had expected to find the lads in a jovial mood but they were looking quite downcast. Turned out the Sky High cocktail bar was closed for repairs. Not a great start to the tour but I know we'll rise above it. Looking round I could see some of the younger guys sharing very emotional farewells with loved ones. Lucky their wives weren't there to witness it. But it was good catching up with the boys, sharing a few laughs and passing the time with a bit of duty-free shopping. I managed to find a beautiful anniversary present for Ros — a 24 packet gift box of Peter Stuyvesant Extra Milds — which I know she'll love. Before we knew it our boarding call went out and the lads, looking smart in official team blazers, boarded the flight to Hong Kong. Of course, the days of teams getting completely rat-faced on international flights are long gone and now a far more professional approach is taken, with most of us completely drunk before we even get on the plane. Nonetheless it was a pretty uneventful trip, the only real disturbance being caused by Warney who somehow managed to set off the smoke alarm in the dunny on four separate occasions. Eventually I drifted towards sleep, my last thought being that just a few days from now Warwick Todd would be battling it out at the crease in the famous baggy green. Shit, I knew I forgot to pack something.

Wednesday February 14

Hong Kong to Mumbai

The flight from Hong Kong to Mumbai also passed without incident, with most of the boys playing cards, working on their autobiographies or just resting. Barely 24 hours into the tour there's already a great sense of team unity and togetherness amongst the lads, a fact I remarked on to new boys Hados and Funky when I went back to visit them in the economy section.

A few hours later we touched down in Mumbai, to be greeted by a massive crush of locals at the airport. For those who have never been to India it's almost impossible to describe. It's like another country. People pushing and shoving, waving autograph books. And then there's the beggars. I know you're not supposed to encourage them by donating anything but one tragic, emaciated little figure caught my attention as he stumbled forward and held out his withered hand, no doubt seeking a few rupees. It was only after I tossed him a two dollar coin and kept walking that someone pointed out he was Chairman of India's Cricket Board of Control. All I can say is I hope the money is well used.

Warney offers the traditional namaste greeting at Mumbai airport. That small dot on his forehead is just a nicotine patch he forgot to take off. I also offer a traditional greeting.

4

No matter how many times you visit India it's always a huge culture shock to see the level of poverty and overcrowding. I remember my first time here back in 1989 on a youth tour. Driving from the airport we could see these rows and rows of bundles along the side of the road. We asked our driver what they were and he said 'people'. We found it almost impossible to believe that anyone could live like that, curled up under rags on the side of a highway, and it was only when we got our driver to swerve and clip one of them that we realised it was true.

The ten-minute drive to our hotel ended up taking half an hour thanks to a huge traffic jam (and the fact Warney spotted a KFC and insisted on stopping) but we eventually arrived and managed to check in. We have our own floor and security guards are stationed at all doors and lifts with pretty clear instructions to not let anyone in unless they are armed with an autograph book.

I must say a major improvement in touring life is the fact we now all get our own rooms. Not so many years ago this was a luxury reserved for only the captain and anyone wearing an Australian Cricket Board blazer. Sharing with fellow players used to be a real lottery and if you scored someone who was, say, a neatness freak it could quickly drive you mad. You know the sort of bloke, always wanting to make the beds and empty ashtrays. But more than just being annoying, the wrong room-mate could actually affect your form. If, for example, you were sharing with a heavy snorer it could mean quite a few sleepless nights. I've shared rooms with a few big snorers over my career, including Mark 'Tubby' Taylor, Tim 'Maysie' May and of course the legendary Darren 'Boof' Lehmann. Boof was so bad that on the last Ashes tour of England he became the first Aussie player in history to actually be fined for snoring. Admittedly it wasn't just the noise level but the fact he was doing it in the middle of a pre-match meeting that attracted the penalty, but either way, single rooms are a major improvement.

After a quick shower and change of clothes I headed back downstairs to meet up with a few of the boys. In the past, players on a tour of India have tended to hole up in their hotel rooms but nowadays a lot more of an effort is made to ensure everyone gets out and down to the hotel bar at least once a day.

Thursday February 15

Today is basically a rest day here in Mumbai, with players being given the chance to recover from the trip and generally acclimatise to the place. We met shortly after breakfast for a talk from our security man Reg Dickason who will be accompanying us throughout the tour. Dicko's basic advice for staying out of trouble was to clear all travel plans with management and only go out in groups. He also suggested we avoid visiting nightclubs with Ricky Ponting. A few other 'housekeeping' matters were covered at the meeting, including medical advice. Everyone is taking malaria tablets and to prevent anyone forgetting our weekly dose we've decided to all take them together every Monday, which should be easy to remember as this also happens to be most of the guys' bath/shower day.

During lunch our ever-cautious physio Hooter produced a food thermometer which, he announced, would be used to test all meals served to the team. Any food not over 60 degrees will be rejected as unfit and sent back to the kitchen. Our lunch passed the test easily, registering 75 degrees, which was a little disturbing as we were having salad. This tour will see a strong emphasis on keeping everyone match fit; bowlers will be weighed at the start of play and at lunch — if more than 5 per cent of body weight has been lost they will be offered intraveneous hydration. Less than 5 per cent and they'll be offered a kick up the arse from Tugga.

This afternoon we flew to Nagpur, a dusty, orange-growing centre of 2 million people, most of whom appeared to be hanging round the lobby of the Pride Hotel when we checked in. Our hotel is comfortable enough by Indian standards with good showers, toilets and beds — unfortunately all in the one room. We're here for our first tour match against India A, which is due to kick off on Saturday, and tonight a team meeting was called to discuss this important opening fixture, as well as general tour rules. In something of a bombshell, our coach John Buchanan announced he was considering an alcohol ban. We were naturally shocked and a little

Her smile is infectious. So too is most of her produce.

saddened, but figured if Bucks really wants to go on the wagon then that's his decision. Imagine our surprise when he explained the ban would be on everyone and last throughout the tour. The only exception would be celebratory drinks at the end of match days, with a midnight curfew! As you could imagine, a fair bit of heated discussion took place and various compromise plans were put forward. Drinking to be banned two days before a match and on travel days. No drinking after midnight before a game or on rest days. Bucks to f*#k off back to Australia. I must say the entire debate was handled with great maturity with everyone contributing suggestions and ideas. In the end a draft drinking proposal was formulated and agreed to —namely, that all members of the squad refrain from drinking on Thursday March 3.

Friday February 16

Well, the holiday had to end and after several days of airline food, acclimatising and general rest it was time to saddle up for our first training session. However, getting into our official gear this morning it soon became obvious that the ACB had stuffed things up yet again, issuing us all with heavy woollen vests, long-sleeved shirts and thick trousers. Perfect for a few hours under the Indian sun, I don't think! We've put in an urgent request for new gear and the ACB are express freighting over a pile of cotton tank tops they fortunately had earmarked for the upcoming Ashes tour.

It felt good getting back into the nets and middling a few balls. Our bowling brigade also slipped into gear well, loosening up with a few overs each. Much of the focus in the local press has been on our front-line paceman Pigeon, but in my opinion the man to watch will be his 'co-star' Dizzy. He's an incredible bowler who has fought to overcome all sorts of injuries and setbacks to get where he is today. Provided there's no unforeseen accidents and our team cortisone supply holds out, the big South Australian looks set to be a match-winner.

We followed up the net session with some long and high ball-catching practice. It was a fairly gentle training run, especially when I think back to those sessions run by our former coach Bob Simpson. Simmo would push you harder and harder, waiting for a player to crack. No doubt his 'finest hour' occurred here in India back in '86 when Simmo pushed Tim Zoehrer so far back that our one-time wicket-keeper found himself caught in a barbed-wire fence. Ziggy wasn't exactly pleased about the event but to be fair, he didn't drop a catch that entire series. Possibly because he contracted tetanus and didn't play another match.

Tomorrow is our first game of the tour, a three-dayer against India A, and at the team meeting tonight we were reminded that it was during this match last tour that Tendulkar hit a double century and set himself up for a big series. Our plan this time around is to attack him hard and destroy his confidence early. Naturally there'll be a few friendly words of 'greeting' when he arrives at the crease, and our quicks have been instructed to bang a few 'welcoming' balls in short. We went through the rest of the India A line-up and devised a similar game plan for each player — actually, it was an identical game plan, except for Laxman who we've decided to bounce first and then sledge.

Saturday February 17

Australia vs India A
Vidarbha Cricket Association Stadium, Day 1

Because wake-up calls are traditionally so unreliable here in India every member of the squad must have some back-up, either an alarm clock or watch. It gets tricky though when you have to adjust to local time, and I got the shock of my life this morning when my alarm went off at 10.00 am! Knowing the team bus left at 9.00, I leapt out of bed in a panic and flung open the curtains only to discover it was pitch black outside. I realised then it must have been the early hours of the morning, a fact confirmed when I saw Warney and Pigeon staggering their way back to the team hotel.

Down at the ground Tugga won the toss and elected to bat, giving us the chance for a bit of time in the middle. For blokes such as myself, Slats, Hados and Lang it would be a much-needed opportunity to work up some form before the first Test. Unfortunately Slats went second ball and Lang was given out lbw to a delivery that was clearly going over his stumps. Fair dinkum, we've been back in this country five minutes and already the umpires are robbing us blind. Things began looking really dire when the normally rock-solid Tugga went for a duck. I was next in and it's always an awkward moment knowing what to say to a player (especially your captain) who's walking off after a big failure. In these situations it's often best not to even make eye contact but something about Tugga's slumped shoulders made me want to cheer him up a little. In hindsight, the phrase 'shit shot mate' might not have been the best choice of words but I was under pressure.

I joined Punter at the crease and between us we managed to see off a quite fierce spell from paceman Ashish Nehra. This bloke was fairly quick and pretty fired up, having six lbw shouts (one before play had even started) turned down. As it turned out, it was the spinners Harbhajan Singh (2–63) and Rahul Sanghvi

Cricket trip canned

Cricket fans who booked a ticket on Warwick Todd's Supporters Tour of England for the 1999 World Cup have demanded their money back after several clients complained about failing to see a single match live. According to one disgruntled tourist, Todd had promised "the best seats in the house" to all of Australia's World Cup fixtures but in the end simply dropped his customers off at a west London pub and told them to watch proceedings on a large TV screen. He was not then seen again for a fortnight.

Tugga offers little assistance as yours truly searches desperately for a missing packet of Winfield blues.

(5–40) who did the damage. I fell to a ball that kept low and was back in the rooms for 52, a good start to the tour and one I really hope to build on, provided the three-match suspension I copped for questioning Umpire Sadashiva's sexuality and eyesight is overturned on appeal. We were eventually dismissed for 291 and by stumps the home team were 1 for 171 with the match evenly poised.

Back at the hotel there was very little in the way of entertainment on offer. Tugga said he had a couple of 'hot' videos we might want to watch but when the boys got to his room the video in question turned out to be footage of his 151 not out against New Zealand last year. We watched politely for a few overs before most of the boys drifted back downstairs for a drink. Lang decided to get a haircut at the Pride Hotel's salon but the owner was too frightened to use the number one blades on him, so Funky stepped in and completed the cut. Let's just say it's a shocker, and the lads took great delight in witnessing the displeasure of our Number 3 batsman.

Sunday February 18

Australia vs India A
Vidarbha Cricket Association Stadium, Day 2

One of the hottest topics in India right now is the ongoing investigation into match fixing and corruption. Every interview we do seems to contain a question about this issue and even though we repeatedly maintain that no Australian player is or was knowingly involved there still seems to be a lot of interest in the matter. Things really hotted up this morning with word that the head of India's Criminal Bureau of Investigation was at the hotel and wanted to see Mark Waugh immediately. I tell you what, Junior looked pretty worried as he went downstairs but it turned out that the bloke was only here to get an autograph for his son.

This morning we recorded our first official (that is, non-alcohol related) illness of the tour with Marto battling a bout of food poisoning. Hooter reckons it must have been last night's chicken tikka masala at the hotel restaurant and was last seen waving his food thermometer at the chef in a quite threatening manner.

India A resumed their innings on 1 for 171 and by lunch had cruised along to 231 without losing another wicket. It was just one of those mornings I guess, with

There's no doubt the Indians love their cricket. This crowd of 110 000 turned up at Eden Gardens two days before the Test began just to watch a final training session.

nothing seeming to go right for us. Both Tugga and Junior dropped catches off Kasper, and Gilly let through 13 byes, most of them off Funky. It's during sessions like this that frustrations can easily build up and it's important for a fielding side to stay switched on. Most annoying was the fact that a decidedly B-grade batsman in the form of Sadagoppan Ramesh was making most of the runs, racing towards a century despite everything we tried. With things getting a little desperate Tugga moved a few of us in close to see if we couldn't unsettle the in-form fella with a few well-chosen words. Now there are many people who mistakenly think sledging is all about offensive or abusive comments but the truth is it's far more subtle. It's about distracting a player, taking his mind off the game. We started with something completely innocuous, asking Ramesh 'How's your wife?' He didn't react and so immediately after the next ball I chipped in 'We all enjoyed having sex with her last night.' I gotta tell you, that one normally gets them going but this bloke was fair-dinkum unflappable. He didn't miss a beat, cruising to a century by lunch. It was only during the break we got word he doesn't speak English.

After lunch Funky came out firing, taking 6 for 91 to skittle the home side. Backed up by two quick wickets from Dizzy we had them all out for 368 just half an hour before stumps. Of course, having to bat for such a short period can often be difficult, especially in fading light and after a long day in the field, and our openers Slats and Hados agreed the main aim was for them both to still be there in the morning. Naturally enough, two balls in, Slats danced down the wicket for a big drive, missed the ball completely and was clean bowled. Tugga was still so pissed off at the close of play he ordered the team bus to leave without Slats, ensuring our opener was in fact still there in the morning.

Monday February 19

Australia vs India A
Vidarbha Cricket Association Stadium, Day 3

From the moment we arrived at the ground this morning you could tell it was going to be a scorcher. Not that you get too many cool days in this part of the world but even by 8 am the heat was stifling.

Luckily we've come prepared for situations like this, with special ice-vests designed to keep the body's core temperature down available to anyone out in the middle for an hour or more. Hados didn't need one and frankly could have gone out to bat in a jumper for all the time he lasted. Tugga didn't last long either, being caught at bat-pad off hot-headed leg-spinner Balaji Rao, who then proceeded to give our skipper quite a verbal send-off. Most of it was in Punjabi or Swahili or whatever the bloke speaks but you could tell it was pretty full-on. Naturally enough Lang, who was at the other end, stepped in to defend his leader, telling Rao he was disappointed at the lack of respect being shown to the office of Australian captain. I don't think those were the exact words he used (and he only used two) but things certainly got a little tense out there.

Unfortunately, by this stage our scoreline was not looking all that healthy. Marto had bounced back from his food poisoning but the umpires ruled that he would have to bat further down the order because he'd spent so much time off the field yesterday. Pretty hard-arsed attitude if you ask me, especially as it was THEIR BLOODY COUNTRY'S FOOD that poisoned him in the first place. Anyway, the upshot of all this is that Warwick Donald Todd found himself at the crease early on the morning of Day 3 batting to save a bit of national pride. Lang was at the other end and we built a solid partnership together, slowly pegging back the home team's first inning's lead. But I tell you what, it was hot out there. Despite the ice-vests and regular drink breaks we were both sweating like pigs. By mid-afternoon I was almost in a trance-like state, completely focused on not getting out and making runs. Even mid-wicket conversations became less frequent. Occasionally I'd stagger down the pitch and say something like 'Let's nail these black bastards', but even this stopped after Lang pointed out I was talking to one of their bowlers. Eventually, though, I pushed a ball through mid-on and took off for a single, bringing up one of my most rewarding first-class centuries ever. I eventually went for 115 and when I stumbled

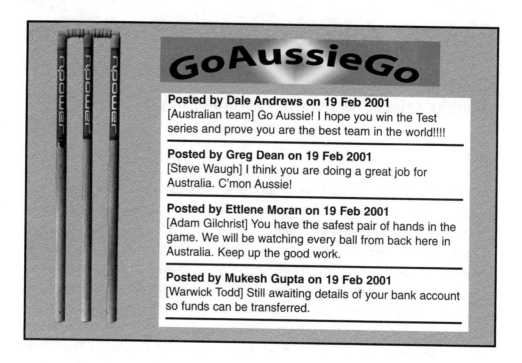

GoAussieGo

Posted by Dale Andrews on 19 Feb 2001
[Australian team] Go Aussie! I hope you win the Test series and prove you are the best team in the world!!!!

Posted by Greg Dean on 19 Feb 2001
[Steve Waugh] I think you are doing a great job for Australia. C'mon Aussie!

Posted by Ettlene Moran on 19 Feb 2001
[Adam Gilchrist] You have the safest pair of hands in the game. We will be watching every ball from back here in Australia. Keep up the good work.

Posted by Mukesh Gupta on 19 Feb 2001
[Warwick Todd] Still awaiting details of your bank account so funds can be transferred.

into the dressing-room our trusty reserves were there with the drinks. Or what remained of them — the bastards had been on the piss since the tea break.

Thanks to my innings as well as some good knocks from Punter, Lang and Marto, we made it to 9 for 365 with the match declared a draw. Celebrations were kept to a minimum as we had to fly out of Nagpur tonight bound for Mumbai. Unbelievably, the flight took off on time (a first for subcontinental aviation) and we were able to share a few drinks on board to mark the end of our first tour match. Despite being seated in the relative comfort of business class we were still interrupted by one very persistent autograph-seeker who simply refused to take the hint and 'piss off'. Not one member of the cabin crew seemed remotely interested in getting rid of this excitable, if slightly malodorous, fanatic and eventually our team manager 'Brute' Bernard threatened to call for the pilot, at which point we were informed this guy was the pilot.

Tuesday February 20

After a fairly late night we were not all that happy about being woken at 8.30 am, especially on what was officially designated a 'day off'. But our sponsors must be looked after and this morning's task involved a massive bat-signing session for Foster's. I'd reckon the average player would be called upon to sign his name at least two hundred times a day on tour, whether it's in an autograph book, on a bat or a piece of clothing. Perhaps the most unusual request I've ever had took place a few years back at a nightclub in London when one eager young female fan requested I sign her breasts! It was the first time I'd ever met Danni Minogue but I was more than happy to oblige. Not so this morning, as the massive pile of bats took over an hour to complete. However, our commitments didn't end here as team management had decided to deal with the massive number of interview requests coming in by organising a 'meet-the-press' morning in the Taj Mahal Hotel night-club, a venue chosen because it was one of the few locations everyone in the team knew easily how to find. The theory was to give the local press two hours with us and then we would hopefully be left in peace for the remainder of the tour. About

150 Indian journos were herded into the room while we players each sat at a table ready to be interviewed, photographed and, in my case, fingerprinted. The session was closely policed by ACB Coporate Relations Manager Brendan McClements, who would blow a whistle every ten minutes indicating that it was time to move on. Most questions directed my way were of a predictable nature: 'Are you happy to be in India?' 'Do you think you can win?' 'Who broke the glass door in the hotel lobby?' Judging from the crowd around him Warney was by far the most popular interviewee, with at least twenty journos crowding around his table. Since arriving in the country Warney has been desperate to change the popular perception that he doesn't like India, going out of his way to say how much he was enjoying

the place. A lot of the local media were quite impressed when our star leggie arrived at the airport last week sporting the traditional red 'namaste' dot between his eyes, seeing this as a sign of Warney embracing Indian culture. Fact is, the red dot was simply a nicotine patch he'd forgotten to take off after the flight over, but it seems to have done his image a fair bit of good. Of course, for every legitimate journo here today there were at least a dozen ring-ins whose only interest was in obtaining players' autographs. I overheard one such 'journo' commence his interview with Pigeon by handing across a notebook and asking 'Could you sign this four times?' (Half an hour later Pigeon was still working on the project.)

Wednesday February 21

I was looking forward to a bit of a sleep-in this morning but as a member of the Australian team on tour you can just about guarantee some idiot phoning you at 7 am. How my wife Ros got the hotel's number is a mystery but she sounded a little upset. Turns out she's going into hospital this week for a minor surgical procedure. It's something we knew was due sometime but didn't expect to be dealing with quite so soon. Naturally it's a personal matter and out of respect for Ros's privacy I won't go into details here but we're confident the liposuction procedure will go smoothly, despite the enormous amount of fat involved. Nonetheless, I'll be relieved when it's all over.

A practice session at the nearby Brabourne Stadium was scheduled for 10 am and so after a quick breakfast I boarded the bus along with the rest of the boys. The short journey was an eye-opening experience as we made our way through Mumbai's jam-packed streets, full of thronging masses scurrying around like ants. Those who recognised us generally smiled and waved, the more enthusiastic of them actually running alongside the bus in hope of a quick handshake or autograph. One very keen bloke could actually be seen out the back window sprinting towards us in the heat, waving and desperately trying to attract our attention. Turned out to be Marto who must have slept in and missed the bus.

After a good net session with Buck and Tugga our fitness adviser Jock Campbell took over proceedings, moving us out of the blazing sun and into the stadium's gym where he set up a training circuit with different stations: sit-ups, push-ups, stomach work and weights. In one corner Funky and Flem began exercising with a boxing routine. Or so we thought. It later turned out they were having a punch-up over who should play next week.

Lunch was excellent, with good helpings of chicken tikka masala and naan, followed up with ice-cream. I spent a fair bit of this afternoon in the physiotherapist's room. There was no one else in there, it was just a good place to sleep off the meal. Back at the hotel we learnt that both Tendulkar and fast bowler Agarkar have pulled out of tomorrow's match with 'injuries'. Piss-weak little shits. Just frightened of losing to a pumped up Aussie outfit if you ask me. The Indian selectors also announced 32-year-old spinner Narendra Hirwani would be recalled for the first Test. This bloke hasn't played since '97 so it came as a bit of a surprise. He was apparently at the recent Indian training camp but most people felt he was only included in the squad to help out with net practice. 'Bit like you, eh Kasper?' I quipped over the dinner table. At which point I was dragged across the dinner table and held down by the throat until security officer Reg Dickason arrived and managed to pull our big Queensland quickie off me. He eventually calmed down and we were both able to share a drink and a laugh about the incident later at the hotel bar.

Some disappointing news awaited me back in my room tonight — apparently cyber-vandals have hacked into my personal website www.toddy.com.au. I guess it was bound to happen, being such a popular and well-visited site. (We had over 40 hits last year.) My manager back in Australia sent me through a copy of the damage, along with an assurance that those responsible for altering my home page would be tracked down and punished.

Thursday February 22

Australia vs Mumbai, Brabourne Stadium, Day 1

During the warm-up this morning Tugga announced we would be resting Dizzy, Marto and Kasper for today's match against the Ranji Trophy champions Mumbai. Play started on time with Pigeon making good use of the early humidity to really move the ball around, taking two quick wickets in the first session. Junior took a great catch diving in slips and somehow the ball managed to wedge in the webbing of his left hand (top pic). It was one of those freak catches where the ball just seems to stick and it reminded me of a similar one I took fielding at short leg a few years ago (bottom pic).

Unfortunately for Junior, he ended up splitting the webbing on his hand and required stitches at a local hospital. Bad news from the medical team there, he won't be able to bat tomorrow. Good news, he was still able to sign an autograph for them all.

Shortly after lunch we had Mumbai struggling at 5 for 82 but by this time the ocean mist had cleared and things became a little harder for our bowlers. Despite the difficulties Pigeon looked like he was in full Test mode, firing stony stares and the odd word of 'encouragement' at their middle order. Warney struggled a little and to be honest looked like a man under a bit of pressure. When he eventually broke

through to dismiss tail-ender Jajin Paranjape, Warney trailed the young player halfway to the boundary with a massive verbal send-off. I haven't seen such a blistering attack from our star leggie since the time that twelve-year-old kid took a photo of him smoking in New Zealand. No doubt the experts will be quick to pounce on this minor incident and write Warney off as a 'spent force' but those of us who know the bloke well realise he'll be saving a little something up for the first Test. In fact, he's been working on a bouncer to stop batsmen advancing towards him and he tried it out with great success today. Admittedly it was only on the team bus, but his accuracy was spot on and come the right moment it could be a potent delivery.

Eventually a few more wickets fell, one each to Flem and Funky who are still locked in battle for a Test berth and another two to Punter, leaving the home side on 9 for 328 at stumps.

Dinner tonight was a quiet affair with most of us pretty knackered after a long hot day in the field. Of course there's no such thing as a 'night off' for touring cricketers these days and after dinner Buck suggested we go back over the day's play, analysing various statistics with the aid of our team computer. It's a pretty amazing piece of technology which, at the touch of a button, can provide detailed information such as a player's susceptibility to a certain type of bowler or how many times a batsman played and missed outside the off-stump. At the touch of another button it can also show you what Cameron Diaz looks like in the nuddy but that particular program is strictly reserved for rest days.

Friday February 23

Australia vs Mumbai, Brabourne Stadium, Day 2

The bad news at breakfast this morning is that Junior may be in serious danger of missing his first Test match in eight years. His left hand is still so heavily bandaged that Lang was having to help cut his toast. Mind you, he often does this anyway. The good news is that last night Funky visited the local Crawford Market where he miraculously managed to find a jar of Vegemite. Its contents were out of date by four years and clearly not fit for human consumption which made it the perfect gift for Warney.

Down at the ground play got under way with Mumbai declaring on their overnight score. The total of 328 was not huge but, as Tugga said in his pre-match address, it's important we take things slowly and adapt to the local conditions. Unfortunately, Slats fell for 11, his third failure of the tour so far. Cricket's a funny game — our big-hitting opener has only faced 55 balls for a total of 27 runs in 3 innings, yet anyone in the team will tell you his footwork and stroke play have been impeccable. He walked back into the rooms after being dismissed this morning and smashed a table to pieces with one perfectly timed drive. Hados also went cheaply, getting a very questionable lbw decision which saw me in a mad scramble to get kitted up and out the door. As you can imagine, the Mumbai boys were pretty fired up by this stage and I was greeted with a few 'pleasantries' from the close-in fieldsmen. Verbal warfare is part and parcel of the game and moves to stamp it out are in my opinion misguided. I've been sledged at the crease ever since the day I began playing. In one of my very first matches I remember the wicket-keeper asking 'How's your wife? I rooted her last night.' Naturally I didn't take this seriously — I was only eleven and the keeper involved was my brother Don — but it's been non-stop ever since. Mind you, the Indian's use of the tactic is pretty primitive. For a start, a lot of what they say is in Urdu or Punjabi so you only get the odd word. It's like 'blah blah blah poofta blah blah blah soap blah blah blah showers blah blah'. It's not so much unsettling as confusing. Anyway, I managed to see out the first few overs and was just getting the feel of the pitch when a ball kept a little lower than expected and I was trapped leg (nowhere) before wicket for 15. At this point Tugga came to our rescue with a beautifully made 106 that took our final score to an almost respectable 203 just a few minutes before lunch. Looking back on the morning I think we all struggled with the sharp swing and turn the Mumbai bowlers managed to extract. Over lunch we continued to struggle with a dry and chewy lamb korma that I suspect had been left over from an abandoned '96 World Cup fixture.

Things didn't get much better after the luncheon interval as our bowlers struggled to take wickets. Instead of an early breakthrough we watched as the Mumbai openers cruised effortlessly to 83 without loss at stumps.

As you can imagine, it was a pretty sombre bus trip back to the hotel. But one of the strengths of this Aussie side had always been our ability to bounce back. One 'bad day at the office' wasn't about to destroy our confidence and by the time we reached the hotel a bit of team spirit was beginning to resurface. A lot of this comes down to mental toughness, being able to visualise the positive in any situation. I remember back in 1989 when I rammed my Pajero into a bus shelter on the way home from training and was subsequently charged with drink-driving, reckless driving and failing to stop at the scene of an accident. Naturally there was a blaze of negative publicity and calls for my sacking and it pretty much looked like my entire world had collapsed. But I stayed positive throughout the ordeal and sure enough, a few weeks later, I signed a lucrative sponsorship deal with ARB bullbars.

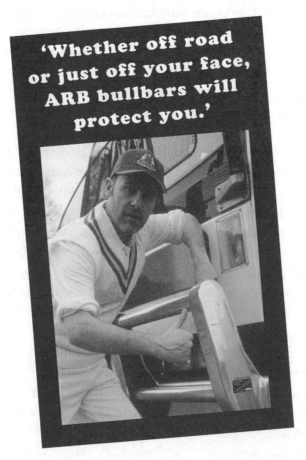

'Whether off road or just off your face, ARB bullbars will protect you.'

Loading up for the long trip ahead.

(Above) Huge crowds surround our team bus hoping to get a glimpse of an Aussie player in the flesh . . .

(Right) An opportunity I'm always happy to provide.

I never miss an opportunity to help promote our sponsor's products.

I always believe in backing up our bowlers wherever possible.

My charity work is about never losing sight of the kids.

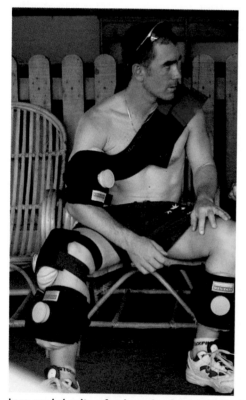

Lang needed quite a few icepacks after his big innings. As did I.

Saturday February 24

Australia vs Mumbai, Brabourne Stadium, Day 3

Sure enough, the tide turned for us this morning. Refreshed by a good sleep we came out firing to have the home team back in the pavilion for just 191 runs. Warney was back to his best, bagging 7 for 56 in a sensational spell of bowling that will hopefully silence some of his many critics. There's no doubt our blonde leggie cops a lot of scrutiny from the press and whenever he fails to take a few wickets these self-appointed 'experts' are quick to write him off. No doubt this morning's spell will have a few of these pundits hurriedly rewriting their newspaper articles. (Regrettably, it was too late for me to do so. Despite an urgent call from the rooms at lunch my column for tomorrow's edition of the *Times of India* has already gone to print featuring the headline 'Warne Worn Out'. I'll simply have to deny any knowledge or keep out of his way for the next week.)

We were set 317 to win in just under two sessions, not an easy task but still achievable given the depth of talent in the Aussie dressing-room. Unfortunately that's where most of us spent the afternoon, slumping to 6 for 141 before stumps mercifully ended the match in a draw. With a top score of just 34 it was obvious that no one really came to terms with the conditions. Our footwork was slow, Slats and Punter both being stumped, and when the crunch came no one really put their hand up.

After the match we were asked if anybody wanted to go out for a drink and everyone put their hand up. But our coach Bucks had other ideas, calling an urgent team meeting back at the hotel. It was here he gave us all a verbal rocket, saying we weren't switched on and that it was time for us to knuckle down. He said a few other things but they were a little hard to hear over the noise of Slats's new Bon Jovi CD. I fear some heavy training sessions are on the way!

After three long days of cricket it was good to get back to our rooms, put the feet up and watch some cricket on the telly. It's virtually on non-stop here in India: month old Pura Cup matches, the Pakistan vs New Zealand one-day series, all shown in their entirety. I suspect the Indians don't actually have a phrase for 'highlights package'. At least it's a good way of getting off to sleep.

Sunday February 25

The agenda for the squad today included a 'mystery activity' that had us assembling excitedly in the hotel foyer at 9.30 am. Turned out to be a training session. This to me is a serious misuse of team management's power. Predictably enough we were put through a pretty gruelling work-out under the ever-watchful gaze of Buck and our fitness adviser Jock Campbell down at the Wankhede Stadium. Upon arrival, the ever sadistic Campbell laid down the law, instructing us to do six warm-up laps of the ground then ten lots of 100-metre sprints followed by another four warm-down laps. I can tell you, everyone looked a little unimpressed except for Pigeon who simply looked confused. He whispered to Gilly 'Does he want us to run or what?' Training sessions a few days before a Test match tend to take on extra significance, as the players try to duplicate match conditions. Which perhaps explains Dizzy's sustained and vicious spell of short-pitched bowling. Either that or he just doesn't like me.

Back at the hotel Tugga announced we'd received an official invitation to visit Bombay's notorious red-light district where woman work in cages to satisfy their clients. Quite a few of the guys expressed interest in going until it was explained

Digging Deep

By GEOFF SEYMOUR

A proposed housing development project on the outskirts of Newcastle is to be investigated by environmental authorities after calims that several of the home sites are located on a former toxic waste dump. The development, "Bonavista Heights", was heavily promoted by Australian cricketer Warwick Todd who yesterday admitted the housing site was contaminated. "Listen mate, you dig deep enough and you'll find mercury and lead just about anywhere in the world. They're naturally occurring minerals and simply part of the unique living environment that is Bonavista Heights..." All pending a full investigation.

this was an official charity exercise, not an informal team bonding activity, at which point most of the boys decided they'd give it a miss.

The team meeting this evening was one of the longest and most intense I've ever attended, as we attempted to dismantle the opposition's strengths and weaknesses. Every Indian player was put under the microscope, their technique analysed and game plans formulated. After almost two hours of close scrutiny the best we could come up with was the fact that Tendulkar could be a little supsect against short-pitched bowling (plenty of bouncers for him!) and that Ganguly was having an affair with a well-known actress called Nagama (Punter to work on an impersonation of his wife).

The traditional pre-Test team dinner was an enjoyable affair, giving everyone the opportunity to relax and let their hair down before the big match got underway. During dinner Tugga organised for us to be shown a motivational tape he'd put together featuring a compilation of what he believed were the twenty greatest batting performances of the past decade. It was a good idea in principle but perhaps a little narrow in focus as the only batsman featured was Tugga himself. Before we'd even got to his 1995 tour of the West Indies quite a few of the lads had snuck out for a drink at the bar.

Monday February 26

We woke this morning to the news that the Don had passed away. The announcement officially came through at 2.15 am so fortunately most of the squad were still up enjoying a few 'quiet ones' at the hotel bar. I was personally shocked and greatly saddened. It was only just a few weeks ago Ros and I had auctioned off a signed portrait of Sir Donald that would have, as of today, been worth a hell of a lot more

Attempting to visit the Don.

money. Life can be cruel sometimes. I remember visiting Sir Donald once, a few years ago at his home in Adelaide. To be honest I found him a little stand-offish, especially as I'd made quite an effort to get there. You try climbing an eight-foot high front fence in the middle of the night. All I got for my efforts was a letter from the Bradman Trust warning me not to come within a mile of the premises ever again. (Perhaps I could auction this off? Must get onto e-Bay.)

Just a few years before his death we were thrilled when the great Sir Donald Bradman paid us a surprise visit in the dressing-rooms at Adelaide oval. Knowing what a huge fan I was, Pigeon kindly grabbed my camera and fired off a few shots. This was the best of them.

Team management were angry to learn this morning that a rival local beer called Kingfisher have used a photo of us Aussies on our stop-over in Hong kong in a newspaper ad. The ad claims we are drinking Kingfisher (as opposed to official tour sponsor Foster's) which is total crap and casts serious doubts on our professionalism. Let me state clearly for the record, we were all drinking Foster's at that team breakfast.

Apart from this hiccup I think everyone is feeling pretty good about the first Test tomorrow. The only real concerns are Junior's finger and Slats's lack of form. But he'll come good — Slats thrives on the big occasion, you should have seen him at the karaoke night last Saturday. And Junior's hand is definitely improving. He'll have a fitness test today and the only real worry is that with his stitches he may not be able to field well. Still, that never stopped us selecting Dizzy.

At the team meeting this evening Tugga reminded us we haven't beaten India in India for 32 years and there's no doubt the odds are against us (9–2 according to Junior).

Tuesday February 27

Australia vs India
1st Test, Wankhede Stadium, Day 1

This is our mountain, let's climb the peak
Beat India in India and then we will speak
Those words in the dressing-room, a beer in each hand
'Under the Southern Cross' we do stand.

(Steve Waugh, read before play, Day 1)

A strong feature of our '99 World Cup win was team poetry, with each member of the squad being invited to address the boys with a few well-chosen words of inspiration before each match. Tugga kept the tradition going today and I think he pretty much summed up our mood.

Warm-ups in India are fairly brief. All you've really got to do to raise a sweat is leave the hotel lobby. Back in the dressing-room after our warm-up we all observed a minute's silence for the Don. I think it was the first time in a decade I've seen Slats turn a Bon Jovi CD off. As a further mark of respect we had intended to wear black armbands onto the field but a representative from tour sponsor Foster's complained that this would obscure their logo so we had to scrap the idea.

There's a lot of superstition and ritual in an Australian dressing-room. Players like to sit in the same seats they've always occupied, which is of course not always possible if you've smashed it to pieces after a previous failure at the ground. We also like to prepare for play in exactly the same way. Junior prefers to sit by himself, staring across the ground to obtain a feel for it. Flemo listens to heavy metal music through his headphones. Hados tends to walk around naked. The rest of us just try and stay as far away from Hados as possible.

We won the toss and decided to send India in, which was a gutsy move from Tugga, but he felt there was enough grass on the pitch to offer our pacemen a bit of movement. Both teams stood side by side for another minute's silence just before play which wasn't easy for Pigeon and Dizzy who by this time both had up a full head of steam. When play finally started our pacemen hit the home team with a fiery spell of fast bowling, dismissing them for just 176 runs. Warney also bowled magnificently, taking 4–47, his best figures against India. The only real resistance came from Tendulkar who made 76. He was a little cautious early but after lunch

Slats in the nets before play showing some youngsters the finer points of batting.

And attempting to do the same during the first Test.

switched up a gear and belted us all over the ground. In the end, though, Pigeon got him with a perfect delivery.

Slats took his dismissal well.

With just a session left to play it was important we didn't lose any wickets but unfortunately Slats's run of bad luck continued when he went for just 10. As our opener trudged back towards the rooms there was a frantic burst of activity, with every breakable item of furniture or equipment locked away and plenty of soft cushions placed around the room.

To our suprise Slats seemed pretty composed, walking calmly through the dressing-room and into the toilets. Of course, this was just the calm before the storm and it wasn't long before we heard the familiar sound of plumbing fixtures being torn from a wall. Hooter eventually managed to calm the big New South Welshman down with a few words and a tranquilliser dart.

We finished the day on 1 for 49, a magnificent team effort from all concerned. If the day could be summed up by one event, it was late in the Indian innings when Funky ran all the way round the boundary to take Flem a drink down on the fence. It was Flem of course who kept Funky out of the team and he was bowling the sort of fast off-spinners that Funky specialises in yet here they were, in the heat of a Bombay afternoon sun, sharing a drink. It's what makes this team so great.

Wednesday February 28

Australia vs India
1st Test, Wankhede Stadium, Day 2

We've got them on the mat
But let's not stop at that.
Let's go out there and bat
In the famous baggy green cap hat.

(Damien Fleming, read before play, Day 2)

We were up early this morning, a little stiff and sore but keen to continue our battle with the Indian team. Bad news at breakfast — Flem has come down with food poisoning. The doctor thinks it may have been something he drank yesterday.

Down at the ground there was a good-natured and appreciative crowd of about 20000, along with another 10000 whistle-blowing dickheads, waiting for play to begin. Unfortunately our great play yesterday quickly became a distant memory as early wickets tumbled. A few experts questioned the wisdom of selecting Junior with a broken finger but his injury didn't cause him any real problems at the crease, possibly because he only faced one ball. With Punter also out for a duck I found myself walking to the crease with just 63 runs on the board. Despite all the training and net sessions nothing quite prepares you for your first few overs in a Test series and I don't mind admitting I struggled a little adapting to the conditions. Hados was at the other end and took most of the early strike while I slowly played myself in. But on just 16 an innocuous delivery from Singh managed to get through and disturb the furniture. It's moments like these when it's natural to give vent to your frustration with a muttered aside or half-whispered curse. How, then, my words could later be described by the match referee as 'a sustained and vocal assault on umpire David Shepherd' remains a complete mystery.

We slumped to be 5 for 99 when Hados was joined by Gilly just before lunch. The two left-handers then set about turning the match around with a magnificent partnership.

' . . . a sustained and vocal assault on Umpire David Shepherd'.

Hados was in great touch, defying those critics who said he couldn't play spin, with a chanceless ton. As usual, on 100 he raised his bat, crossed himself and kissed the coat of arms on his helmet. Gilly was slightly less demonstrative, merely raising his bat and adjusting his box, but the sentiment was still there. Our keeper's century was the second fastest in 124 years of Australian Test cricket.* Gilly finally fell shortly before tea, stumped on 122 when a ball from Harbhajan Singh beat him, bounced off keeper Mongia's gloves and back onto stumps — an innings of pure class ended by pure arse. A little resistance from our tail-enders took the final score to 349, a lead of 173.

We only had an hour or so left to bowl at the Indians but these short periods late in the day can often be a valuable opportunity to take wickets and sure enough, Dizzy and Pigeon obliged, knocking over Das (7) and Ramesh (44). To top off a great day, Dizzy forced Mongia from the ground with a possible broken finger. Of course, no one likes to see anyone get hurt on a cricket field (unless of course they're Arjuna Ranatunga) but this was not only a major psychological blow for us, it also brought Tendulkar to the crease for one final over. He was lucky to survive a couple of big shouts from a pumped-up Pigeon, including one before he even faced a ball, but managed to survive the brief spell with his wicket intact.

After a long day on the field everyone was pretty exhausted and so after an early meal most of the boys headed back to their rooms for a quiet night. Some of the younger guys like to watch video tapes of their recent innings, which could be seen as an example of their dedication and professionalism, but the truth is they just enjoy watching themselves bat. I opted for a bit of in-house adult movie entertainment which turned out to be a complete waste of money. A$17.50 to watch a couple of Indian chicks competing in a wet-sari competition — I think I've been away from home too long.

* The fastest of course being Jack Gregory's 67 ball ton against South Africa in 1921–22, a match now believed to have been fixed.

Thursday March 1

Australia vs India
1st Test, Wankhede Stadium, Day 3

It's the first Test and we're up to day three
It's now our chance to make history.
Let's maintain the pressure and never stop
Until from the winners trophy we do sop.

(Mark Waugh, read before play, Day 3)

I tell you what, if we thought the Indians would go down without a fight we were wrong. Led by a typically aggressive Tendulkar they dug in and by lunchtime were only 50-odd runs behind our first innings total. Despite this the mood at lunch was surprisingly upbeat, partly due to the excellent lamb biryani on offer. Dizzy bowled with real fire all morning and there was some excellent fielding from all the guys, including Slats who clearly had Dravid caught at square leg off Flem. Imagine our surprise when the video umpire Narendra Menon ruled that the ball had hit the ground! Naturally Slats was a little upset by the decision, as it called into question his honesty and integrity as a player, but after a few friendly words with umpire Venkat (to be accurate, just two words) and a bit of a chat with Dravid (the same two words, only louder), he let the matter drop. Imagine then our further amazement when Slats was told he had to meet with the match referee Cammie Smith after play! Perhaps fired up by the injustice of all this, we came out after lunch even more determined to take the upper hand. And it wasn't long before the breakthrough came, Tendulkar caught after the ball hit Lang's shoulder at square leg and bounced to Punter at mid wicket. I guess it was just one of those freakish shots that can go either way. I remember playing the Windies a few years back in Adelaide, Boonie was fielding at short leg when a miscued shot bounced off his stomach and cleared the long-on boundary for six. But luck

Slats had a few friendly words with umpire Venkat.

was with us today and once Tendulkar trudged off, the rest of the team fell pretty quickly to be all out for 219, leaving us just 47 runs for victory.

During the break Tugga gave us a pretty serious talk about the perils of chasing a small target and the way Australia has failed to do this successfully over the years. It was a good talk and a pity we couldn't hear much of it but by this stage the CD player was cranked up pretty loud and some of the guys had already launched into a few verses of the team victory song. Sure enough, we reached the required target in just seven overs, recording our sixteenth consecutive Test victory.

Immediately after the winning runs were scored we all emerged from the rooms and did a lap of honour for not only the Aussies in the crowd but also the generous Bombay fans. One of the biggest roars came when Warney performed the namaste, a traditional Indian greeting. Mind you, there was an even bigger roar when I dropped my pants, a traditional Australian greeting. The only sour note came during the presentation ceremony when India's captain Sourav Ganguly was loudly booed. Frankly I found this both unfair and unsportsmanlike, but Pigeon refused to stop.

I tell you what, the feeling in our dressing-room afterwards was incredible. Everyone was hugging and jumping on top of each other. Blokes' managers were jumping on top of other blokes' managers. As part of team tradition we all gathered around the physio's bench where Ricky Ponting stood to lead us in a rousing version of 'Under the Southern Cross'. It's a stirring anthem and the words are well known to all. However, in the hands of Punter the tune remains a complete mystery. It was still hard to believe we'd won the Test inside of three days but looking round at the boys you could tell everyone was really pumped. We were also pretty exhausted after such a huge effort, none more so than Lang who was covered in bruises, having taken twelve sharp blows to the body at short leg (and one more in the dressing-room when Hooter accidentally fired a champagne cork in his direction). Gilly was so pumped with the win and his great innings that he announced he would be wearing his baggy green cap for an entire week, a practice normally reserved for only his underwear.

The celebrations were unfortunately cut short for Slats who was forced to meet with match referee Cammie Smith for a disciplinary hearing where he was let off with just a warning. Smith later explained one of the reasons he didn't come down harder was Slats's previously good disciplinary record. The other reason: he was scared shitless the fiery New South Wales opener might go him with a bat.

Despite the enormity of our win and the boys' natural desire to celebrate, Tugga reminded us to keep proceedings under control as we still had another two Tests to play.

Friday March 2

Don't remember a thing.

Saturday March 3

With our next match not due to start until Tuesday today was officially declared a rest day, and looking round at a few of the seedy faces at breakfast this morning I figured this was a pretty good idea. There's no doubt we Aussies enjoy celebrating a win and the past 24 hours remain little more than a blur. I vaguely recall being at a nightclub and a report this morning in the *Times of India* suggests that a bit of a disturbance took place there but no one is named specifically. Apparently someone — an Aussie — threw an ashtray through a window and according to an eyewitness the perpetrator was 'unsteady on his feet, his eyes were glazed over and red and he smelt of intoxicating liquor', a description that quite frankly could fit any one of us in the Australian squad.

Speaking of the papers, there's been a flood of criticism over here for Slats and his behaviour in the last Test, with commentators calling for everything from a hefty fine to life imprisonment. Naturally Slats is making a point of not reading any of these articles but it must be difficult because I've been cutting out the worst ones and leaving them under his door. The local press has also been savage on the Indian team. Gavaskar called them 'pussycats' in his column in the *Times of India* while the *Asian Age* ran a front page photo of Nagama (Ganguly's alleged lover) with the caption 'Was Sourav's mind somewhere else?' Looking at her tits most of the boys figured 'yes'.

After breakfast a few of the lads, including Tugga, Lang, Pigeon and myself, took a tour of Bombay where we visited the gold and silver bazaars as well as the Dhobi ghat at Mahalaxmi, which is the world's largest out-door laundromat. To see these Indian women, bent double in the noon sun, bashing clothes against a rock makes you realise just how good we've got things back at home. I don't think Ros has hand-washed an item of clothing in ten years. She just bungs everything into the Whirlpool front-loader, hits the switch and heads off to aqua-aerobics.

My precious baggy green is definitely 'hand wash only' after Ros managed to shrink it in the Whirlpool.

Sightseeing is never easy in India because of course the moment people recognise you a massive crowd forms and the dreaded autograph books come out. In these situations I've learnt the only way to deal with people is a firm but polite 'f**k off' but even then the truly persistent fans keep following. After an hour or so of being jostled you have no choice but to seek the safety of the team hotel. We did manage one quick stop on the way home, the local McDonald's where we ordered up big on Maharajah Burgers that, instead of being made from beef (which is sacred) are made from lamb (which is inedible).

Despite several tours of India, a sight you never quite get used to are the child beggars. Outside our hotel is this ten-year-old kid who has been waiting with his family — brother, two sisters and dad — every day since we've been here. Each morning I've been sneaking a small package of food out of the hotel — fruit and biscuits, which are destined to be thrown out anyway — and selling it to them at a very reasonable rate. I guess I've always been committed to helping out under-privileged kids and I do a lot of charity work back in Australia. Naturally it's very low-key and I keep myself very much in the background of **WARWICK TODD'S** Care for Kids **WARWICK TODD** Foundation. We basically take kids in need of help or support or even just a holiday and arrange for this to happen with funding from the foundation. Of course, being such a well-known and successful figure as I am, the tall poppy syndrome means that other people are always trying to cut me down. You wouldn't believe the obstacles that have been put in my way over the years. Like the Taxation Department which investigated the charity after claims that the only two kids who had been helped, supported or taken on holiday were my own. Based on this one technicality they tried to shut the foundation down but I'm pleased to say we're still in there fighting. (If you feel like helping out, remember all donations are tax deductible — cash only.)

Sunday March 4

Check-out mornings are always frantic but fortunately the Taj Mahal Hotel put on extra staff this morning to handle the mass exodus. In all there were eight employees behind the desk, one in charge of check-outs while the other seven worked frantically to add up our mini-bar bills.

The usual delays at the airport saw us sitting round the departure lounge for several hours with nothing to do but play cards and read the papers. According to the local press, animosity between the Aussie and Indian teams continues to simmer. Several Indian players have apparently complained that no Australian went to see how Mongia was after he took that blow on the hand from Dizzy. The fact is, we didn't need to — his hand was obviously stuffed. And we wanted to watch it again on the scoreboard replay. Besides, how many curry munchers went to see how Lang was the twelve times he got hit on the body at short leg? Speaking of our Number 3, he's still being treated for the bruises he sustained during the first Test. In the search for a speedy recovery Hooter has made him alternate between ice-filled baths and steaming hot ones. Given the hotel plumbing over here it's a sensation most of us experience on a daily basis anyway. Also on the injured list is Gilly who is receiving ice treatment for a slight strain to his abductor muscle. But on a more positive note for our vice-captain, he's just signed a personal contract with our tour sponsor Foster's, cashing in on his amazing innings. While I'm happy for Gilly I'd be lying not to say I'm a little disappointed with Foster's for overlooking my constant support in the promoting of their product. I show up at all their boring sponsor functions, wear my official cap wherever possible, and I was once arrested outside a nightclub in Victoria for allegedly chucking a half-full can of THEIR PRODUCT at a moving car.* Still, if Gilly's temporary form is considered more valuable than my long-term commitment then so be it.

Eventually we boarded our flight and took off for the capital New Delhi. One of the unique features of Indian air travel is the mad scramble as you land when every passenger desperately tries to be the first one off the plane. Before the wheels had even touched the tarmac there was a stream of passengers racing down the aisle, luggage in hand. It wouldn't be such a concern except for the fact half of them were our flight crew.

* The charge was later dropped after the magistrate agreed with my lawyer's claim that Warwick Todd would never knowingly throw away an unfinished can of beer.

The Taj Palace Hotel in New Delhi. I suspect the word 'palace' may be used a little liberally here in India.

A short bus trip took us to our new home, the Taj Palace Hotel. (I suspect the word 'palace' may be used a little liberally here in India. Basically anywhere with electricity and an inside dunny seems to qualify.) The boys were looking forward to a bit of R & R but to our horror an official government reception had been organised to welcome us to the capital. The only interesting moment came when Tugga stepped forward to shake hands with the mayor's wife, only to be told it is not correct protocol to touch a female in public. 'You should have told Punter that last night at the nightclub!' I quipped before an ACB corporate relations manager suceeded in dragging me outside.

I tell you what, nothing quite prepares you for the choking pollution of New Delhi. It's like a thick cloud of choking smog hovers over the entire city. A lot of offices and restaurants round here now have a policy of asking smokers to go inside before they light up. And talk about crowded. Even our hotel is surrounded by high-rise apartments with people packed on top of each other into tiny little boxes. A few of the younger boys said it reminded them of the Cricket Academy in Adelaide.

After a few days off it was back onto the paddock today for a lengthy training session. On this tour our training regimes are being led by a new fitness adviser, Jock Campbell. The great thing about having Jock as part of the team is the fresh ideas he has about staying match fit. The bad thing is he wants to implement a lot of them. A few hours of sprints, push-ups and star jumps left most of us breathless and exhausted. Fortunately the net session was a little less demanding. After training today Warney gave a bowling clinic for the young 'would-be' Test cricketers who hang round our nets and help field. Hopefully Kasper and Flem got something out of it.

Monday March 5

There's no doubt about the press over here, if they can't find a good story to write about then they'll make one up. This appeared on the front cover of just about every paper this morning.

Players 'got sex to fix games'

A former cricketer has named 23 prostitutes he claims helped corrupt Test stars.

By **GARETH STEVENS**
LONDON

The scandal surrounding international cricket corruption took a new twist last night amidst revelations that top players agreed to throw matches in return for sex with Australian prostitutes.

A key witness to the ICC corrpution inquiry has claimed that the women were used by illegal bookmakers to entice many of the world's top players, including Australians, to throw matches or perform poorly. Many of the deals were allegedly arranged in Australian hotels according to London's The *Observer*. British investigators probing match-fixing are said to be very keen to speak with the players involved within the next month. The player making the allegations, former Pakistani batsman Qasim Omar, has provided a list of 23 prostitutes to chief investigator Sir Paul Condon. All the women were Australian except for one Pakistani and one who was Chinese. The

Australian Cricket Board's special investigator Greg Melick said he had no knowledge of Australian players being involved in any such activities although he was aware of such claims. According to Omar one Australian bookmaker lavished gifts, money and free sex on players who would do as he asked. Additional incentives for playing poorly came in the form of jewellery, watches, fountain pens and bottles of spirits. He even identified one Australian batsman who deliberately underperformed because he needed money to finish renovations to his house.

For me this was the final straw in what has been a long and hurtful smear campaign. Let me make one thing absolutely clear, the woman in the photo is from an Indian aid agency for which I have recently been doing some work. She's a sort of social worker, practically a nun. We'd been at a nightclub discussing child poverty when obviously some low life with a telephoto lens thought he'd make a name for himelf. Publishing this photo and the accompanying headline was unfair to both me and Sister Ginger. But it's the sort of thing I've had to get used to, ever since this whole match-fixing and bribery scandal broke. For months now I've had my name mentioned in connection with shady deals and illegal actvities. I tell you what, to have one's honesty questioned is a terrible thing. To have one's word doubted can be very hurtful. To have one's bank statements examined — that's bloody frightening. But that's exactly the sort of thing that has been happening since the ICC started its investigation into match fixing. Yes, I admit to once having accepted money from a bookmaker, but as I explained to ACB special investigator Greg Melick, it was a totally innocent event. Without wanting to rake over the past again, here are the facts. In 1994 we were staying at a hotel in Colombo, Sri Lanka, when I bumped into a bloke at the bar who wanted to know if he could ask me a few questions. I naturally assumed he was a journalist. I guess when he offered to pay for the drinks I should have become a little suspicious, but by this time I'd already told him a few things about our team line-up and various players' form. Next thing I know he's handed me $5000. When this story finally broke a lot of journalists and so-called 'experts' began screaming 'bribe!' which just goes to show how ignorant they are of how things work on the subcontinent. The fact is, it is *customary* in countries like India to exchange gifts. Flowers, rice, incense, small cash payments — all this is perfectly normal, as I explained to the investigating team. I told them everything I knew. Yet still the slurs continue.

Still, I wasn't about to let the press ruin my day and shortly after breakfast I joined most of the other guys on the bus for a sightseeing trip to the Taj Mahal. It's a four and a half hour journey over pretty rough roads but as anyone who has been there will tell you, it's well worth the effort. The place is hundreds of years old and was built as a present by some maharaja bloke for his wife Mahal. As one of the man-made wonders of the world I'd put it right up there between the Great Pyramids of Egypt and EuroDisney. One member of the squad who didn't make the trip was our star leggie who stayed behind in New Delhi to film a TV commercial for SPC microwaveable baked beans and spaghetti. Some of your cricket 'purists' don't like the idea of Test players making ads but the fact is we all need to supplement our incomes in whatever way is possible. Over the years I've fronted campaigns for cordial, lawn sprinklers, retractable awnings, towbars, hormone replacement

Warwick Todd says
'Hit hair loss for six!'

OZ-FUSION

therapy, boat insurance and National Liver Awareness Week. Just before leaving for this trip I even found time to complete a magazine shoot on behalf of a new sponsor Oz-Fusion, promoting their tufft-by-tufft™ hair-loss reversal treatment.

At the team meeting tonight we briefly discussed tomorrow's three-day tour match against the Board President's XI. Interestingly, India's captain Ganguly has included himself in the team line-up which we hope will give us the opportunity of really crushing the beleaguered skipper. Since the first Test he has been savaged in the press over his leadership, or lack of it, and according to reports he is yet to even arrive in Delhi! Hearing stuff like this only makes you more grateful for the excellent captains Australia has had over the past few years, each with their own unique style. Guys like AB who could go two months on a tour without saying a word to you. Then there was Tubby whose approach was far more 'hands on'; he was the sort of guy who'd visit every player in their room for a series of one-on-one discussions about the match ahead. (The only time AB ever visited my room was to borrow a bottle opener.) I still remember vividly the day it was announced in an ACB press release that 'Mark Taylor has resigned as captain of Australia'. We were stunned. It was the first time we'd ever heard him referred to by his actual name. This was of course the beginning of a new era under Tugga whose captaincy style is also unique. He's a great thinker and always searching for new ways to motivate the team. During the summer of 1999–2000 he decided to start inviting guests to our pre-game dinners, inspirational figures who could pump up the boys. In Brisbane it was Pat Rafter, who was fantastic. Down in Hobart we were joined by four members of the 1948 Invincibles who were also great, despite three of them nodding off during dessert. After this Tugga let us organise the speakers and in Perth Lang arranged for Kim Hughes and Rechelle Hawkes to come along while in Melbourne, Warney scored Rex Hunt and Sam Newman. I was offered the job for Sydney where my surprise guest not only held the attention of the entire table, she also danced upon it.

She not only held the attention of the entire table, she also danced upon it.

Tuesday March 6

Australia vs Board President's XI
Ferozshah Kotla Ground, Day 1

The day began with controversy when we woke to learn that Slats was in trouble for comments he made to Sydney radio station 2WS last night about the now-infamous Dravid catch. According to Slats the whole thing has been totally blown out of proportion but under ICC rules he is technically forbidden from commenting on a matter once it has been referred to a match referee. Personally I know what it's like for Slats, having your name dragged through the mud then being prevented from giving your side of the story. The very same thing happened to me back home last summer after a disputed catch I took off Brian Lara. Once again, the matter was referred to a match referee so I'm prohibited from writing about it here.*

Shortly after breakfast we boarded the team bus and arrived at the Ferozshah Kotla Ground which takes its name from the adjoining 600-year-old ruins of Delhi's original fifth city. Most of the stones have been removed from the city walls and, judging from the quality of last night's sleep, been used to stuff our mattresses at the Taj Palace Hotel.

Tugga won the toss and elected to bat at which point Ganguly seemed to lose all interest in the game, placing himself on the boundary and looking generally disinterested. At one point I swear I even saw him chatting on a mobile phone.

We got off to a somewhat shaky start, with Slats adding to his general woes when he was dismissed for just 19. I followed soon after for just 12, out lbw to a ball that clearly

I'm all for batsmen congratulating each other on a big knock but frankly this was going too far, especially when you consider Hados had only just reached double figures.

* Except to say the catch was legitimate and Lara's a dirty cheat.

41

took an inside edge onto my pads. When the umpire's finger went up I was genuinely stunned and instinctively I held my bat up so that he could see the mark where the ball hit. According to some commentators I may have held the bat a little close to his face (the bloke was obviously short-sighted) but at no stage did I 'brandish the bat in a threatening manner' as was later alleged. Fortunately Punter and Tugga both made centuries and, helped by a quick-fire 62 from Junior, we made it to 8 for 413 at stumps.

I simply held my bat up so that he could see the mark where the ball hit.

Dinner tonight was of a very high quality and most of the boys enjoyed tucking into some pretty decent curries. I say 'most', as Warney would have nothing to do with the local fare, contenting himself with a basket of bread rolls. There's no doubting it, our star leggie is a living miracle, having survived for thirty years on toasted cheese sandwiches, bread rolls, chips, sauce, spaghetti bolognaise, nachos and Burger Rings. And that's just breakfast.

Wednesday March 7

Australia vs Board President's XI
Ferozshah Kotla Ground, Day 2

I must say, security here in India is pretty full-on and everywhere the team goes we're shadowed by military types with submachine guns and forced to walk through metal detectors. I haven't been subjected to such close scrutiny since the early days of the Australian Cricketers Association.

Another blisteringly hot day greeted us this morning although according to weather reports a cold snap actually brought rain to Calcutta last night which is of course the venue for the second Test. Knowing India's concept of pitch covers tends to involve six blokes holding an umbrella, we could be in for a slightly green wicket there.

We resumed play on 8 for 413 and our tail-enders managed to take the score along to 451 before the home team commenced their innings. Most of our focus was on Ganguly who came to the wicket with the score on just 12. First ball from

PRIVATE PROPERTY
Edited by KATRINA DEMSTER and TONY MEEK

Good Todd!

Aussie batting legend **Warwick Todd** and his (ex?) wife **Roslyn** have put their 4 bedroom townhouse (pictured) on the market. The big-hitting batsman is off to England in June but hopes to secure a sale before heading off on his Ashes tour of duty. Chez Todd features two bathrooms, a gymnasium (presumably unused), four separate bars and a massive "trophy room" featuring twenty years of cricketing memorabilia — mainly photos of W. Todd wielding the willow on cricket fields round the world. One anonymous real estate agent described the room as a "gargantuan monument

to self-ego, with life-sized portraits adorning every wall not covered by pennants, trophies, ribbons and mirrors". Phew. The house also has its own outdoor bar (presumably very well used) and is offered for private sale. Expect offers around $400,000 — roughly Toddy's match fine total to date!

Kasper the Indian captain got the faintest of edges and by some stroke of luck it carried. Unfortunately, it carried to Marto who failed to grasp the opportunity. In the end Ganguly made 40 but this was more through luck than any real form. There's no doubt the Indian skipper is under a fair bit of pressure over here for his elitist attitude. While his team-mates stay at the four star Hotel Broadway (in one of the most polluted areas of Delhi) he is staying at our hotel. In all my years of cricket I can't think of a situation where an Australian captain has stayed somewhere other than with his team, except of course when he's been unavoidably detained in a police lock-up.

Lunches in India tend to be fairly plain: chicken and rice with a bit of ice-cream thrown in. Today's was a little more interesting; the ice-cream was actually thrown into the rice but we were too hungry to complain.

A solid afternoon spell from our bowlers had the President's XI all out for 221, with the honours shared between Kasper, Funky, Flem and even Junior who snared two wickets. As a bowler Junior is often overlooked and I reckon this comes down to his undemonstrative manner. As a batsman he's well known for this feature, making a duck and merely shrugging his shoulders as he casually wanders off. It's the same problem when bowling; when Dizzy or Pigeon appeal it comes out as a full-scale, down-on-the-knees, guttural scream. The best you'll get from Junior is a turn of the head towards the umpire and a raised eye brow. It's never going to convince anyone.

It was interesting that for a lot of the day Tugga stood at square leg and handed over the captaincy reins to Punter. This has always been a feature of Tugga's captaincy, sharing the leadership role and actively inviting suggestions from other players. It's a very different approach from that taken by his predecessor who often did not seem to appreciate contributions from his team-mates. I remember once at Headingley a few years back, Tubby was fielding in slips and I wandered across between overs and suggested he place a man at backward square leg. Well, you should have seen the look he gave me! It was like I had no right even being there. Which was perhaps true — I was not actually selected on that tour and just happened to be at the ground as part of a supporters' tour I was leading. But I still think my input was valuable.

We decided not to enforce the follow-on so as to give us a bit of time at the crease and at stumps we were 1 for 53, with the out-of-form Slats on 24 not out. I guess we're all hoping he might finally get the chance to score some runs tomorrow.

Thursday March 8

Australia vs Board President's XI
Ferozshah Kotla Ground, Day 3

Well Slats did get to score some more runs today. Two of them, in fact. With our big-hitting opener out for 26 it was time for some much-needed batting practice for the rest of us. Junior and I came together mid-morning and settled in for a long, hot session in the middle. I can tell you what, we sure kept our reserves busy with constant calls for new gloves and cooling drinks. At one point our 12th man Pigeon appeared between overs with a new bat which I hadn't actually called for. Turned out it just needed to be signed for some regional sales manager from Kelvinator. These distractions aside, Junior and I both pushed the score along as the home team sweated it out in the field. Well, at least most of them did. Noticeable by his absence was a certain Indian captain who shall remain nameless (it was Ganguly), who could apparently be seen wandering round behind the dressing-rooms talking

Aussies Mount Their Challenge

■ By PETER ROEBUCK

what's this mean? Look up.

good!

5th African?

Suffused with the inner glow that comes from a 1-0 Test lead the Australian team today continued their sub-continental assault on a Board President's XI with an intemperate display of petulance in the edifice that is the Ferozshah Kotla ground.

Todd had his usual boorish interludes as he played and missed in the manner of an errant schoolchild swatting flies en route to less-than-robust 12. Yet whilst occupying the crease he moved with intent and are the feet not merely the brain at work? Eventually the loquacious left-hander elected to lift the pace, charging down the pitch like an enraged Cossack only for umpire Venkat to raise his finger, a task he carries out in the style of a nihilistic gendarme on the streets of Paris leaving Todd to eschew centre stage, cursing and masticating as he went.

boring?

?

are they?

they don't even play cricket!

I was adjusting my box!

I don't mind if journos want to have a go at me, but they should at least be required to do it in English.

45

on a mobile phone. I was eventually out for 78, trying to push the score along and give a few of the other boys a bit of time in the middle. As usual Junior decided to think only of himself, notching up 162 selfish runs before edging one to the keeper.

Lunch was excellent and I perhaps ate a litte too well because I found it hard staying awake in the dressing-room during the afternoon session. Admittedly Lang was batting so things were a little slow, but I kept nodding off. I tell you what, there's nothing more likely to rouse you from a deep slumber than the sudden shout of 'catch it!' Fortunately it wasn't someone out on the field, just Punter yelling out on the balcony after someone almost knocked over his beer.

We batted all day, ending on 7 for 461 at which point the mercy rule was applied, allowing everyone to head home half an hour before scheduled stumps (with the exception of Ganguly, who'd left for the hotel shortly after lunch). Unfortunately there was no time to celebrate our draw as we had to pack up and head for our next destination, Calcutta, 'a crowded, chaotic cesspit of 12 million people sitting beneath a stifling blanket of pollution'. (And before any residents write to complain let me state that this quote comes from the Calcutta Tourism Bureau.) But like all Indian cities, the people here are totally cricket obsessed. No sooner had we checked into the Taj Bengal Hotel than we were surrounded by fans and autograph hunters. I got cornered in the hotel bar by this absolute weirdo who wanted to know everything about the team, who was playing in the second Test, what the bloody weather would be like . . . it just went on and on. I think the bloke was a little pissed or just plain stupid, because after I'd told him a few things he shook my hand and rushed off, leaving behind quite a pile of money.

Friday March 9

With the second Test just a few days away this morning's agenda involved a 'think tank' session for which we broke into three groups: the quick bowlers, the batsmen, and the two keepers and spinners. After an hour or so everyone got back together and we arrived at some interesting conclusions. The batsmen felt the bowlers have been letting us down with inaccurate and overpitched deliveries. The bowlers felt the batsmen were yet to really come to terms with the slower wickets over here, posting ridiculously low scores which put the pressure right back on them. The keeper/spinner group felt it would be good if we could go go-karting.

We followed the think-tank session up with a solid three-hour workout in which Gilly was passed fit to play. Flem missed a bit of training with a shoulder strain but fortunately he seems to be our only bowler facing an injury. Pigeon and Kasper are looking pumped and ready to go, while I've never seen Dizzy looking fitter, with a niggling hammy, torn thigh muscle, pinched elbow nerve and hairline spinal fracture his only minor concerns.

As usual our training session attracted quite a few local kids keen to see the Aussie team working out. We always take the opportunity of chatting with these youngsters and, when time permits, conducting a bit of a coaching clinic. There's no doubting a bit of good early advice can really help a child along the path to sporting success. I still remember my very first coach, Father McCormack, who used to be in charge of the under-11s before he was defrocked. He would always say to us, 'The three most important things about batting are footwork, footwork, footwork.' He used to have a stutter and we never learnt the other two. Of course, back then we didn't have 'junior development programs' and things like Kanga Cricket to nurture young talent. At my school, would-be players were just lined up, the fat kids sent off to try out for the hockey team and the rest of us given ten minutes in the nets facing up to some psychopathic fast bowler repeating Form Six for the third time. If you survived this they'd present you with a bat and you were on your way. Nowadays Aussie kids get to attend coaching clinics with regular visits from Shield and sometimes even Test players. I've done a bit of this myself and really enjoyed it although I'm not sure I could coach every day. (In fact, as a point of law I can't — the Education Department has a restraining order in force preventing me from coming within 200 metres of any school after I dropped one in a little short and gave a Year 5 student concussion.)

Local kids eager to catch a glimpse of the Aussie team at training often proved a distraction during our net sessions until authorities came up with the brilliant idea of electrifying the fences. This mob of onlookers never bothered us again.

Back at the hotel there was more trouble for Slats who was officially warned by team management not to make any more comments on the Dravid incident. The warning was delivered in person by team manager Steve 'Brute' Bernard and came as quite a shock to Slats as he was on the phone at the time doing a live cross to John Laws.

After lunch Tugga, Junior, Flem, Funky, Lang, Haddo, Buck and I took a five-car convoy on a 47 kilometre trip to visit the Udayan Child Hostel. This facility is funded by Tugga and some of us were interested in seeing the work done there. Others just thought it might improve their prospects of Test selection. The place cares for children of leprosy victims who over here are considered the lowest of the low, although if you ask me match referees must come pretty close. As we drove in, the banner on the fence read 'Welcome Stive Wog'. I must say I admire Tugga and his long-term commitment to places like this. I've personally found charities to be a bit of a two-edged sword back home. I mean, you organise an auction, raise a fair bit of dough to buy a disabled bus and no sooner have you handed over the keys than they're demanding a roadworthy certificate. As I said to the bloke in charge, 'What's the big deal if the brakes are a little dodgy? Most of the passengers are already in wheelchairs anyway.'

Our traditional pre-Test team dinner was held tonight at the hotel restaurant and proved to be a top evening, marred only by yet another security breach. It's unbelievable, there must be 50 guards and police patrolling the foyer yet still a couple of Aussie fans managed to crash proceedings and shout abuse at us all. The hotel manager was all very apologetic when asked to explain how two clearly drunk, foul-mouthed men were allowed into a team function, simply saying that he assumed they were members of the Australian Cricket Board. Fair mistake, I guess.

Back in my room I received a fax from my manager Gabe back home with a copy of a proposed interview for some weekend newspaper magazine. As a popular, high-profile sportsman I get so many of these interview requests that Gabe recently suggested we employ a publicist to help fill in the answers and maybe 'tidy up' my public image a little. He just wanted me to check that her responses were okay and thank Christ he did. She's made me sound like a stuck-up intellectual poof with no mates.

Draft responses for *Under the Spotlight* article on Warwick Todd, Australian cricketer

What are you reading?
~~'Europe: A History' by Norman Davies~~ The ABC cricket magazine

What do you need more of in your life?
~~Tranquillity~~ Foster's

Best place to spend a weekend?
~~At home with the family~~ Playing golf with the boys

Favourite meal?
~~Sashimi~~ Steak

Who is your greatest inspiration?
~~The people of East Timor~~ Ian Chappell

What word sums up your attitude to life?
~~Unequivocable~~ Guts and determination

What sound do you never wish to hear again?
~~A child crying in hunger~~ HOWZAT!

Saturday March 10

Today is the Hindu festival of Holi, marking the end of winter, and outside the Taj Bengal Hotel there were great celebrations with people throwing coloured water and dyes over each other. From my balcony you could even catch the distinctive smell of marijuana in the air, a scent I've not experienced since we last shared a hotel in Auckland with the New Zealand one-day team.

Slats had a meeting with match referee Cammie Smith this morning, at which he was given a one-match suspended ban for making public comments on the Dravid incident. He was also fined 50 per cent of his match fee for the upcoming Test. If you ask me, this is quite ridiculous and yet another example of how the game of cricket is in danger of being over-policed. Telling players what they can and can't say off the field! Even on the field, you've got match referees viewing tapes and picking players up for the most minor indiscretions. Believe it or not, I was once fined $3500 for simply spitting! Can you imagine an AFL or league player being punished for such a normal function? Sure, in my case I was spitting on Daryl Cullinan but that's a mere technicality.

Training today was typically intense as you would expect the day before a big Test. Flem, Funky and Kasper are still competing for a place in the side but the rest of us look pretty settled. As well as the usual onlookers there was a fair media contingent watching our workout this morning and over lunch quite a few of us took

We players rarely read what is written about us.

time out for interviews with various Aussie journos. On a long overseas tour such as this you get to know the 'media pack' pretty well and they're generally regarded as part of the touring party, being invited to many player functions as well as enjoying many of the privileges that players are offered. They don't get drink cards, of course, but apart from that they're pretty much 'part of the team'. I think it's fair to say I've always had a good relationship with the press, possibly because they're often looking for a negative angle and I've always had the knack of providing one. Of course, like most of the guys in the team we rarely bother to read what's written about us.

After a short gym workout we had the rest of the afternoon free and quite a few of the guys headed off to meetings with their managers who have been over here stitching up deals with Indian businesses. Warney has just done a TV commercial for SPC microwaveable baked beans while Gilly is set to launch a clothing range here later this year along with Dennis Lillee. Tugga, Pigeon, Gilly and Punter are also busy writing columns for Indian newspapers. Some people dislike the idea of Australian cricketers making commercial arrangements such as these but the fact is we've all got to supplement our incomes and prepare to one day earn a living outside of cricket. Over the years I've undertaken many business ventures with various degrees of success. My cricket-themed restaurant in Adelaide did quite well until the bloody Bradman Foundation lawyers got all aggressive and demanded that 'Don's Place' cease trading immediately. Ros and I also ran into legal battles when we tried opening a boarding kennel out the back of our house in Brisbane. We built 40 state-of-the-art pens and dog runs only to be shut down by neighbours complaining to the council about the noise. Fortunately it wasn't a total loss as the buildings were able to be modified and we now run a private nursing home facility.

> **DON'S PLACE**
> Adelaide's most popular cricket-themed restaurant!
> From the laid-back ambience of the Bradman Bar to the sumptuous splendour of Sir Donald's Dining Hall, it's the only place to eat for the discerning cricket fan.
> Tasteful. Elegant.
> Foxy barmaids Thurs-Sat.
>
> CLOSED

The team meeting tonight was positive and well received by all the boys. Tugga spoke about the pressure facing India, the fact that this is the equivalent of our Boxing Day Test and it's our chance to really break them. Buck then took the floor and reminded us not to look at what lies at the end of the rainbow but rather what is on the road ahead and that way we'll avoid floating in midstream with our heads in the sand and asleep at the wheel. It certainly gave us something to think about.

Sunday March 11

Australia vs India
2nd Test, Eden Park, Day 1

It's time now for action, our task it is clear,
To tie up the series with a big Test win here
Let's not take a risk, the best way to beat 'em
Is to pick me in the side instead of Kasper or Flem

(Colin Miller, read before being omitted from the team, Day 1)

We all woke this morning pumped and ready for the task ahead, knowing how important this first day would be. Down at Eden Park there were 75 000 screaming Bengalis (and that was just in the press box. Is there anyone in this country not accredited as a journalist?) ready for the battle to begin. Kasper got the nod ahead of Funky and Flem. A bit of gamesmanship from Ganguly took place even before play began, with Tugga being kept waiting inside the boundary for the Indian skipper to walk out for the toss. The cheeky bastard eventually emerged but there was not a word of apology. To top this off, after the toss (which we won) Ganguly didn't even wait to walk off with Tugga as is customary but wandered off on his own. Now I'm no puritan but you've got to have respect for the fundamental traditions of this great game. You toss, you shake hands, you have an awkward interview with the weakest member of the official television commentary team, and then you walk off together.

Fortunately we stuck it up the dhal-diners by getting off to a flying start. Slats raced to 42 when he was caught behind by a ball that obviously clipped his pad. In fact, the red mark on his pad was so clearly visible it was half an hour after he shoved it down the dunny before the evidence disappeared. Hados and Lang then negotiated us safely through to the tea break, the big Queenslander going in on 93 not out. He was reluctant to enjoy a quick 'cold one', under the misguided impression that there was a job still to be done but with only 7 runs to get we convinced him a couple of beers would simply ease the symptoms of those nervous nineties. He was out fourth ball after tea for 97.

We were still in a pretty strong position but cricket's a funny game and it wasn't long after that that off-spinner Harbhajan Singh caused a near riot by taking a hattrick. Singh had Punter plumb lbw, Gilly not quite so plumb lbw (the ball pitched outside leg *and* clipped his bat) and then Warney caught off an obvious bump ball. Warney rightly stood his ground while *local* umpire SK Bansan referred the matter to *even more local* third umpire Sameer Bandekar who deemed the catch fair. It was an extraordinary scene at the ground, with 75000 fans screaming, setting off fireworks, blowing trumpets and lighting fires. And all this was before the decision came through. Afterwards things just went nuts. It was in this cauldron I found myself with Dizzy, attempting the difficult task of steadying the Aussie ship. Understandably the Indian team were pretty pumped up (Ganguly was even back on the field) and keen to finish us off. I managed to take most of the strike and we made it through to the last over when a quick single brought Dizzy to the striker's end. Sensing a kill, and with only a few balls to go, the home side moved in close, really increasing the pressure. It's at times like this that tail-enders need a little support and so I went down to Dizzy and said, 'Forget the score or how many balls to go, just concentrate on the next delivery. It's going to be either a bouncer or a yorker, get in behind it and keep your backswing short.' To which the lanky South Australian paceman simply nodded and replied, 'Say that again'. Communication problems aside, we made it through to stumps on 8 for 269, not a bad result given the outrageous hattrick of earlier this afternoon. The whole country's gone mental over it and Harbhajan Singh looks like becoming their next President. Honestly, this is a bloke who not long ago was investigated by the ICC as a suspected chucker! If you ask me it might be time to reopen the inquiry.

Monday March 12

Australia vs India
2nd Test, Eden Park, Day 2

It's tough here in India and it's gonna get tougher,
But let's guts it out and make the Indians suffer
For the heat and the crowds and the real dodgy tucker
And making us play a turban-headed chucker.

(Warwick Todd, read before play, Day 2)

There's no doubt about it, India is a true test of character. The confronting, over-populated environment of noise, smell, pollution, heat, hostile crowds and appalling food. And it's even worse when you get outside the Australian dressing-room.

Dizzy and I took the score to 8 for 383 by lunch. It was one of those extraordinary partnerships where you keep expecting a wicket to fall but it simply doesn't. The boys told me later that back in the dressing-room no one was moving, partly because of the old cricketer's superstition, partly because most of them had nodded off. I reached my century mid-afternoon and I've gotta say it was a truly special moment, knowing Warwick Todd was back in form. I punched both hands in the air, saluted all sections of the ground that hadn't yet been torched and came dangerously close to hugging Dizzy (the big paceman would have decked me for sure). Whether it was sheer fatigue or a momentary lapse of concentration I was out soon after for 110 and we ended our innings on a very respectable 445. I tell you what, I was knackered after spending most of the day at the crease and the first thing the boys did when I walked back into the rooms was throw me in the spa. It would have been nice if they'd filled it with water first but I still appreciated the gesture.

Now it was up to our bowlers to see how they could perform on what was a pretty flat, dry pitch. I gotta say, there's nothing quite like the feeling of walking onto a cricket field with the Aussie team at the start of an innings all proudly wearing our baggy green caps. I'm not embarrassed to say I treasure my cap and have been known to wear it for days after a big win. I was once actually told by a journalist there were rumours going round that I've worn the baggy green while making love! I naturally denied the suggestion adding that even if it was true my wife Ros was hardly likely to have told anyone. To which the journo replied, 'The story didn't come from her.'

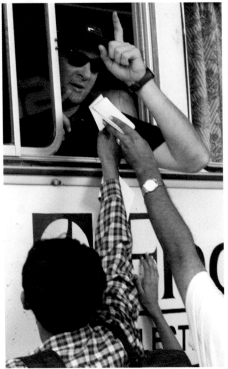

Junior hit upon a brilliant idea in Nagpur when he announced all autographs would now cost one US dollar. By the end of the day he'd made nearly five hundred bucks.

It was alleged I was smoking — the fact is, mornings can be very cold in Calcutta.

Lunch — Day 3

In India I always take time out to mingle with my fans who often like to thank me by handing over small gifts. How was I to know the kid in the baseball cap headed a Bombay-based betting syndicate?

Sourev Ganguly's wife and girlfriends enjoy the action from their specially reserved seats at Eden Park.

Training is interrupted as we search for Marto's missing contact lens.

This shot was taken after our record-breaking twelfth straight Test win last year. The triumphant moment was later marred when Tugga, Punter and Magilla were subsequently fined under ACB rule 17.2 for 'not having a prescribed alcoholic beverage in hand during post-match celebrations'.

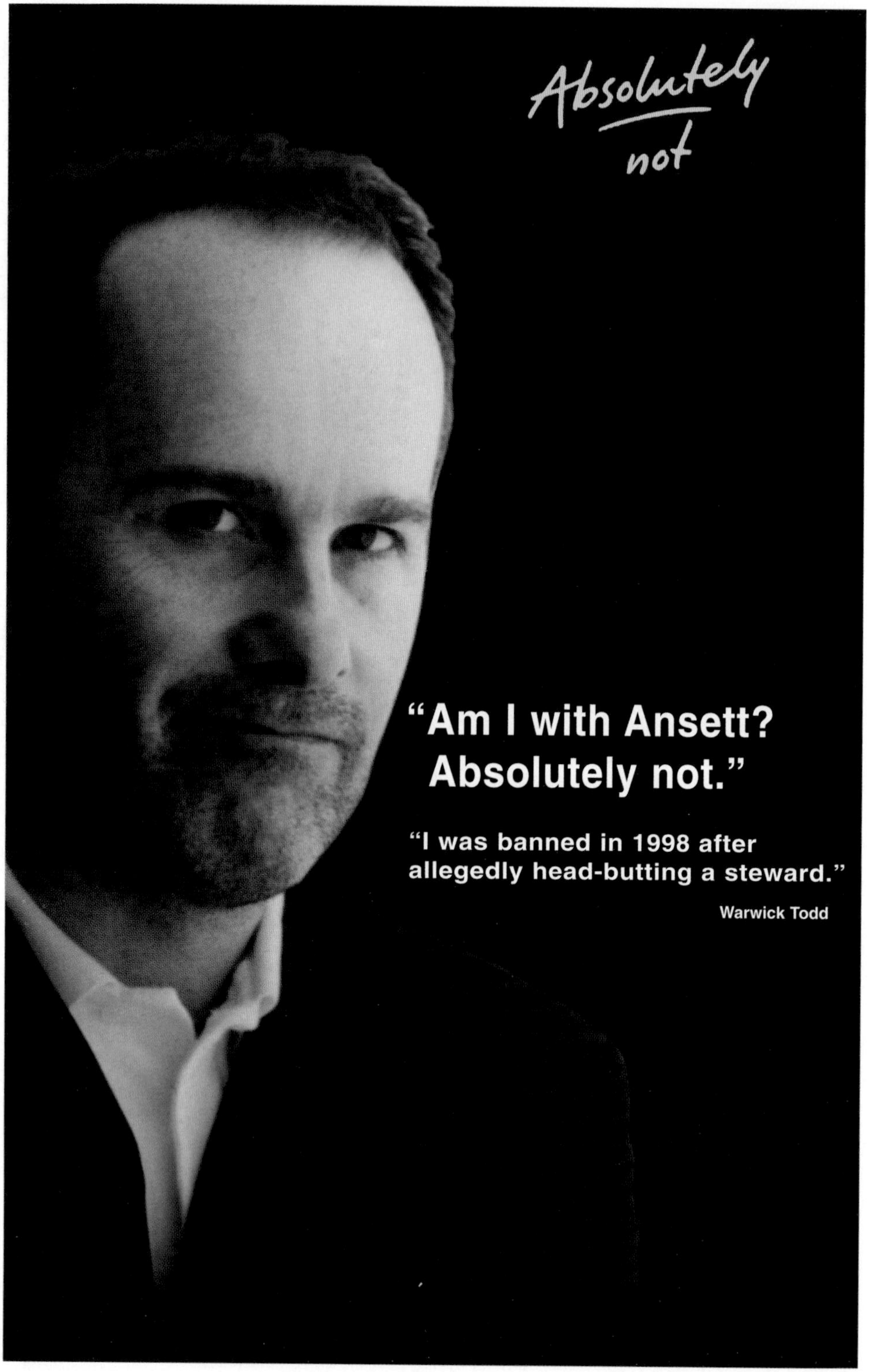
Absolutely not
"Am I with Ansett? Absolutely not."
"I was banned in 1998 after allegedly head-butting a steward."
Warwick Todd

An interesting crowd chant has been greeting us at most grounds here in India, sounding something like 'Ahzi-sah', 'Ahzi-sah', 'Ahzi-sah'. This afternoon it was louder than ever and we finally worked it out: 'Aussie sucks'. Nice to be made welcome.

Pigeon and Dizzy both got early wickets and with the Indian openers back in the pavilion it was time for Tendulkar to face the music. When Pigeon trapped him lbw for 10 the home side looked to be in all sorts of bother. Tugga brought Warney into the attack and he had Ganguly plumb lbw on zero but *local* umpire SK Bansal ruled in favour of the *local* home-town hero in a decision that could only be described as *local*. Or shithouse.

It felt good to score another century for Australia . . .

Fortunately the beleaguered skipper didn't last long and on just 23 was heading for the dressing-room (his own private one apparently). One heart-stopping moment occurred late in the day when a skied catch caused Dizzy and Tugga to both run for the ball. All of us still carry vivid memories of that sickening collision between the two Aussies in Sri Lanka, a collision that hospitalised them both. Interestingly, Tugga later viewed the footage but Dizzy was adamant he didn't ever want to see it, a position he managed to maintain for almost a year until one night he was at

. . . and the boys couldn't have been more excited.

home watching *Funniest Home Videos* and it came on. As it turned out, the boys avoided another head-on and we ended the day with India slumping to 8 for 128, struggling just to avoid the follow-on.

After a few cold ones with the boys back at the hotel I opted for an early night, exhausted after such a big day on the paddock. But before going to sleep I made a point of ringing Ros, knowing she'd be very excited about my big Test century. Unfortunately she hadn't been able to watch the innings (it was *Ally McBeal* night) but promised to catch the highlights package tomorrow.

Tuesday March 13

Australia vs India
2nd Test, Eden Park, Day 3

Our Father who art in heaven,
Hallowed be . . .

(Matthew Hayden, read before being pelted
with cricket balls before play, Day 3)

We woke this morning to find an in-depth analysis of yesterday's play from Buck shoved under our doors, detailing the percentage of scoring shots played by every batsman and breakdowns of each player's on-field performance. I was particularly pleased to receive such a lengthy document as I'd only just run out of toilet paper.

We were pretty keen to finish the home side off and, thanks to some fine bowling from our pace contingent, we had them all out for 171, just 55 minutes into play. Tugga had no doubts about enforcing the follow-on and we went out onto the field pretty pumped, sensing our seventeenth straight Test win. Despite some early resistance Das and Ramesh both fell in their thirties, bringing Tendulkar to the crease with his team placed precariously at 2 for 97. It was during his first over that I managed to cut off a sharp drive, stopping the ball with one hand and returning it to Gilly behind the stumps so quickly that the cocky little Indian was forced to take last-minute evasive action. Now I certainly didn't expect any pat on the back for this, it's all part of the general team fielding effort, so you can imagine my anger when one journalist later described the incident as 'an uncalled for display of petulance'. And you can imagine my even greater anger when I looked up the meaning of the word petulance. As it turned out Tendulkar made only 10 runs, the same score as his first innings, which led a lot of us to ask 'What were the odds of that?' (60 – 1, according to Junior.) An eerie hush fell over the stadium as Tendulkar walked off, the crowd's mood perhaps being summed up by one young fan who chucked a water bottle at the defeated batsman. At this stage India were 3 for 115 and clearly struggling. When Tendulkar went it was as if India's heart had been ripped out, its hopes vanishing into the Calcutta haze.

When Ganguly came to the crease Tugga immediately went on the psychological attack, posting eight men on the off side and just one on the on side, an obvious taunt to the embattled Indian skipper that he is only capable of scoring on the one side. Just in case this point was lost I repeated it verbally on several occasions, along with several new 'pleasantries' I'd taken the trouble to learn in Urdu. Ganguly seemed amazingly unruffled by any of these and it was only during the drinks break that I learnt he doesn't actually speak Urdu. So much for my attempt at bilingual sledging. Despite looking set for a big innings Calcutta's home-town hero

was caught behind just short of his half century, leaving only Laxman between us and a big series win. But wouldn't you know it, the nuggetty little right-hander dug in, racing to a half century in rapid time. Warney copped a fair bit of stick from him, going for 22 in one over. Shortly after this I suggested to our legendary leggie that he 'go round the wicket'. Warney suggested I 'go and get f*#ked'. These frank exchanges of views are a useful and valuable part of the game. Laxman raced to a century, backed up by Dravid, and at the end of play India were 4 for 254, still 20 runs behind our first innings total. We realised that these two batsmen are probably the only thing standing between us and our first series victory in India in 32 years.

Warm applause for Laxman's century.

Wednesday March 14

Australia vs India
2nd Test, Eden Park, Day 4

It's time to stand up for the old baggy green,
Knock over their wickets like a champion team.
Let's play it hard but in a sportsmanlike fashion
And give these curry munchers an absolute thrashin' . . .

(Michael Kasprowicz, read before play, Day 4)

Today had its good and bad features. Breakfast, for example, was most enjoyable. From there things just went downhill. No getting away from the fact, it was a very tough day for us here at Eden Park. A record fifth-wicket stand of 357 between Laxman (275*) and Dravid (155*) took India to 4 for 589 at the end of play, a lead of 315. We took the new ball early and threw everything at them but nothing seemed to work. Warney got smashed around, rarely bowling his flipper or wrong 'un, just his leggies and the occasional bouncer. By the first drinks break even Gilly had to stop shouting 'bowled Warney' as it was starting to sound sarcastic. There's an old rule — in a crisis always turn to your great players. So why Tugga threw the ball to Slats and Punter remains a mystery. Both got carted around, as did yours truly, whose medium-pacers proved no trouble for the in-form Indian batsmen. I did get one ball to beat Dravid and from where I was standing he looked pretty plumb. But umpire SK Bansal disagreed and in my disappointment at having such an important wicket turned down I understandably uttered a passing comment in the batsman's direction. Imagine my surprise to be informed during the luncheon interval that I had been cited for making racist comments! Sure, Warwick Todd plays it tough, but when it comes to racially offensive remarks I draw the line and it's just so typical of a bloody Indian umpire to claim otherwise.

As the day wore on Laxman and Dravid seemed unstoppable, piling on runs with complete ease. Tugga tried everything but nothing seemed to work. Most skippers rely on advice from their keepers and throughout the afternoon you could often hear Tugga ask Gilly questions like 'How hard is Pigeon hitting the bat?' ('Not that hard'), 'Is Warney spinning it far?' ('Nuh'), 'Where the f*#k's Toddy?' ('Buggered if I know'). When Dravid reached his century he saluted the home dressing-room then pointed his bat in anger at the TV commentary position where several of their

Neither Slats nor Punter managed to pick up a wicket but
Punter did later take out our team best new beard competition.

local 'experts' had been questioning his place in the team. The crowds over here
are very statistically knowledgeable and would applaud every milestone: Laxman's
highest Test score by an Indian, the highest score made in a Test in India, the
slowest drinks cart — it didn't take much to set them off. What was particularly
impressive was the degree of concentration shown by Laxman and Dravid. Nothing
we said or did would distract them. References to their parentage, casting doubts
on the strength of their respective marriages, comments relating to matters of
personal hygiene and of course questions about their distinct lack of heterosexuality
— nothing phased the bastards who both ended the day well and truly not out. It
was the first time we Aussies had gone a day without taking a wicket since the West
Indies in 1999. Looking back over all the sessions I think we only had six appeals,
and only two of those were genuine.

Understandably, no one felt much like drinking or celebrating this evening, which
makes you wonder why we were still in the Taj Bengal Hotel bar at midnight. The
mood was definitely downcast with a few of the boys already looking defeated. But
with one day's play still to go I remain confident we can knock over the Indians
and take the series.

59

Thursday March 15

Australia vs India
2nd Test, Eden Park, Day 5

Yesterday was tough, and we've got some work to do,
But if we stick together as a team we can come through.
Let's not sky the towel, we can win this bloody game,
If we just accept the fact that our bowlers were to blame.

(Ricky Ponting, read to a mixed reaction before play, Day 5)

On the final day of a Test match there's not much a captain need say and when we gathered round Tugga for his pre-match talk he was brief and to the point. Which was fortunate as he was sitting on the dunny at the time.

The first part of Tugga's plan went well with Laxman caught Todd bowled Pigeon in the first session for 281. This was obviously a major breakthrough for us but the post-wicket celebrations were marred by a small controversy which as usual was beaten up in the press over the following days. Let me take this opportunity to clear the matter up. It is *customary* to throw the ball into the air after taking a catch. Most players throw it up, I threw it at Laxman's head. We're really splitting hairs. It was a simple, spontaneous gesture of relief and in no way a 'deliberate and provocative act of on-field aggression' as some 'experts' later claimed. A few overs

Tugga's pre-match address was short and too the point.

later Dravid was run out on 180 and the Indians eventually declared their innings closed on 7 for 657, leaving us a total of 384 runs to make in just 75 overs.

We started well, making it to 0 for 24 at lunch but no sooner had the lamb vindaloo been polished off than the rot set in. Local umpire SK Bansal was standing in his final Test before retirement and decided to celebrate the occasion with a string of dubious lbw decisions. Hados was the first to suffer when on 67 he attempted to sweep a ball from Tendulkar that was clearly spinning down legside. Slats went for 43 and Junior made a duck, courtesy of Bansal's new 'leg vaguely before wicket' ruling. Punter also notched up the dreaded duck, caught off the bowling of Harbhajan. The fiery Taswegian was clearly upset with himself for getting out so cheaply and his lack of form so far on tour but as I reminded him back in the rooms everyone goes through slumps. Some for a few matches, some a season. Tubby Taylor had one for most of the late '90s. I know he'll bounce back.

We read in the paper this morning that so engrossing has play in this Test been that there has not been a crime reported in Calcutta in the past four days. Obviously these statistics didn't take into account the daylight robbery being conducted by Umpire Bansal who managed to adjudge Gilly lbw off the first ball he faced. By the time I suffered a similar fate, out lbw on 24 to a ball that clearly clipped the inside edge of my bat, I was seeing red. I marched up to the bowler's end and let fly at the umpire with a string of abuse about shit home-team decisions from substandard curry-munching cheats lining their pockets with rupees while the game slipped into a hopeless mess of corruption. I was so fired up I didn't realise I was actually

The Indian team rush to congratulate Umpire Bansal.

speaking to English umpire Peter Willey who took it all quite well, later letting me off with a 50 per cent match fee fine and two-month suspended sentence. No one else put up much resistance and it was just a matter of time before we slid to be all out for 212, giving India victory by 171 runs. As you could imagine there was total mayhem when the final wicket fell, with 65000 spectators erupting in a mass of noise, flames and smoke. Mind you, they'd been doing that with the fall of every wicket. I guess it was an amazing victory, being only the third time in history a team has won after being forced to follow on. It last happened in 1981 when Botham led the Poms to victory over Australia and before that was way back in 1894 when England defeated an Aussie team led by the young Bobby Simpson.

Man of the Match was umpire SK Bansal.

Friday March 16

Another day, another hotel check-out, another plane trip. The flight to Chennai was uneventful except for the fact it left late and landed in Goa. A brief connecting flight later and we found ourselves checking in at the hotel. Even though it might sound glamorous, a life of constant touring can easily get you down and some of the blokes never really adjust. I guess I'm lucky because moving around is something I got used to as a kid. Mum and Dad were always shifting house. Generally I'd find them after a few days but the upheaval was pretty constant. It's funny how after a loss you start thinking about getting home and being back with loved ones. A lot of the guys are clearly homesick. Naturally, I miss Ros and the kids but the truth is it's not all bad. Sometimes a separation, a bit of distance, can help put the spark back into an otherwise stale relationship. I remember making this very point to Ros a few weeks after we got married when I phoned her from Sanctuary Lakes to say the golf weekend had been extended. There were definite sparks.

Shortly after we checked into the hotel a team meeting was called. Tugga had arranged to kick things off with a conference call back home to our team psychologist Sandy Gordon but unfortunately he's off work with depression. Sandy's been a major part of our team success over the past few years and used to actually tour with us, conducting very valuable motivational sessions before each match. He did perhaps overstep the mark when he began conducting his own net sessions and now tends to remain based back in Australia ready to help any player out over the phone. There's no doubt everyone's a bit flat, mentally and physically, after yesterday's loss. To have had a series win so close and then to see it slip away has been tough on us all.

As a way of clearing the air Tugga and Buck gathered everyone together this morning for an all-in debriefing session. First up our erstwhile stats guru Mike 'Wendy' Walsh took the floor and went through the entire match detailing the strengths and weaknesses of every player involved. His in-depth analysis included things like the fact we batsmen tried sweeping 11 per cent of deliveries yet the stroke yielded us 22 per cent of our runs while leading to the downfall of 60 per cent of the team. This process took about an hour and a half and at the end of it we were able to draw some pretty interesting conclusions, the most obvious of which was Walshy should not be invited to address any more team meetings. The failure of our bowlers to take a wicket on the fourth day was clearly a concern and Tugga felt it was time to develop a broader bowling plan by putting something down on paper that would cover this sort of scenario. Pigeon, Dizzy and Kasper agreed to get together and knock something up that they could then present to the guys in the next few days.

We've basically got 48 hours to come good before the third Test here in Chennai, as tough a cauldron as you'll ever find. It was of course here that Deano almost died of heat exhaustion in 1987 and Boonie was almost killed by alcohol poisoning in 1996. Not the ideal place for a team who have just spent three hard days in the field. Predictably enough, the Indian press are now falling over themselves to praise the local team while the *Times of India* has described us Aussies as looking 'frail'! Our line-up for the next Test is still undecided with Hados battling a dose of the flu. Our coach Buck has also raised the possibility that we may drop Warney who he said was 'clearly distressed after bowling long spells in Calcutta' and was 'lacking match fitness'. Warney then raised the possibility that we drop Buck whose 'obsession with match fitness is a f*#king pain in the arse'. A full-scale fight looked set to break out before Tugga stepped in and called for a bit of calm, insisting there would be no drastic changes to the team line-up. Mind you, Buck was not the only one to attack our legendary leggie. Bob Simpson, writing in the mass circulation Indian *Sportstar* magazine this morning accused Warney of being overweight and unfit. They're the sort of comments that could be very hurtful if Warney ever read them. (And he will, I left a copy of the article with the worst bits highlighted on his pillow.)

Of course, Warney's not the only bloke under the pump right now — Punter's form has been scratchy (0,6,0) and there have already been quite a few calls for Marto to replace him. Admittedly, most of these calls have come from Marto himself, in the form of anonymous phone calls to Tugga's room and little Post-It notes left on the door of the team bus.

With a fair bit of simmering tension and conflict emerging tonight's traditional team dinner looked like turning into a fiery affair, but fortunately no more harsh words were exchanged. We all ordered room service and ate in alone.

Saturday March 17

Last night was one of those nights you get on tour when you simply can't sleep. Whether it's the heat or the strange surroundings, you toss and turn all night. I tried all the usual tricks like a nightcap and counting sheep before I finally had to resort to something stronger and get out a copy of Mark Taylor's autobiography. Three pages into *Time to Declare* I was out like a light. Any chance of a sleep-in was shattered by the sound of the phone ringing at 8.30 am but I didn't mind because it was Ros. It was great to catch up on all the news

Three pages in and I was out like a light.

from home and just the sound of her voice gave me a much-needed boost. It's funny, when I think back to when I was a teenager girls didn't mean all that much to me. On a list of priorities they probably came in about fourth, behind cricket, cars and drinking. Now as a happily married man all that's changed and I'm not embarrassed to state quite publicly that cars no longer interest me that much and Ros is definitely the third most important thing in my life.

An interesting letter appeared in one of the local papers this morning from a group of Aussie fans who attended the second Test in Calcutta who wrote 'For five days at Eden Gardens my colleagues and I were subjected to a barrage of verbal taunts, food, water bombs and blood-drawing rocks.' My advice to them would be next time don't sit so close to the Australian dressing-room. A few of the papers have also picked up on the widening rift between Tugga and Buck over our coach's suggestion that Warney might be dropped. They're quoting a 'source close to the team' which could only mean Warney. The dispute touches on a pretty interesting issue, the precise role of a coach within the Aussie team. A lot of us senior blokes believe that the selectors choose a team, the captain runs it and the coach is there to help out purely with training and make sure the post-match drinks are kept cool.

A full net session took up most of the morning after which we returned to the hotel for another team meeting where there was bad news on the proposed bowling plan front. Pigeon, Dizzy and Kasper had met the previous night and written a few thoughts down, quite a comprehensive plan apparently, but they seem to have lost it. All they can remember is that it was written on a drink coaster which we've all been asked to keep a look out for. As far as batting went we spoke about the need to show a little more respect for India's feisty young spinner Harbhajan Singh (or 'shower cap', as we've named him). As far as the team for tomorrow went, Tugga announced we would be sticking with Punter and that Funky would be coming in for Kasper. Buck then took the floor and spoke about the recent criticisms of his coaching style, saying if anyone had any problems now was the time to raise them, to clear the air. Everyone assured our coach the team was 100 per cent behind him and he left the room looking rather relieved. At which point the real meeting got under way.

After getting a few things off our chest a bunch of us went out looking for a meal but from what we saw this city seems pretty dead. We struggled to find a decent restaurant, there only appeared to be one or two bars open and just about everything seemed to shut by 8.00 pm. The only person impressed with the place was Dizzy but then he's from Adelaide. In the end most of the boys just drifted back to the hotel to work on their poems.

⊠ *Taj Palace Hotel* ⊠
NEW DELHI

Third Test – Day 1 by Warwick Todd

We came here to win the Border Gavaskar Trophy
This is our chance, let's not atrophy (?) Ian Bothamie (?)
Let's not be put off by the crowd's cheering and yelling
It's no harder to take than Buck's blackboard spelling ← (pause for laugh here)

Let's wear our baggy green caps like a crown
And not (let our fans or team-mates down — look at Punter here

The scorecard is locked at one-all apiece
Let's be the man and remain at the crease
And then we will hold up high the gold cup
And know that Australia   sup?
                            pup?
                            erupt?

fuck it.

Sunday March 18

Australia vs India
3rd Test, Chidambaram Stadium, Day 1

The third Test is upon us, it's time to play ball.
We'll fight for the series and give it our all.
With the old baggy green on our heads proudly sitting,
Pigeon and Dizzy will have the home team a-shitting.
Let's play for our country and win the game truly,
So we can stick it up that dickhead Ganguly . . .

(Warwick Todd, read before play, Day 1)

As the boys gathered round to hear my few words of pre-match inspiration I must admit to the odd butterfly. Funny, isn't it? I can go out there in front of 50 000 people and face an express bowler coming in off a long run-up without a worry, yet addressing a small audience can send me into a panic. Truth is, I've never been good at public speaking. In my younger days I'd often get so nervous and tongue-tied the magistrate would usually just tell me to sit down.

Good news from our quicks — they managed to locate their comprehensive bowling plan that had gone missing the night before. Dizzy was elected to present it to the team. 'Line and length.' Not quite worth the wait but good on 'em for trying.

The ground here in Chennai is surrounded by a moat or open drain and the smell coming off this water is truly revolting. Just driving past this sewer in the bus is enough to make you dry-retch and the look of the blackish-green murky water is indescribable. About the only thing that comes to mind would be last night's soup.

Tugga won an important toss, choosing to bat on the dry, bare pitch, and it wasn't long before our openers took guard, Slats looking quite fearsome with his newly shaved head. With a fair bit of patchy form behind him it was important the big New South Welshman did well and, on a positive note, he smashed the second ball of the day to the fence for 4. On a negative note, these were the only runs he scored, caught by Laxman off the next ball. I guess a lot of our critics would have predicted a major collapse at this point but quite the opposite occurred. In hot and humid conditions Hados and Lang pushed the score along rapidly. Lang eventually went for 35, caught off Harbhajan Singh who celebrated the wicket in a manner that could only be described as 'unbecoming'. Naturally the diminutive Indian spinner received no punishment, in stark contrast to Yours Truly who was handed a $5000 match fine in Calcutta for 'overexuberant' celebrations at the fall of Laxman's wicket. Since when is letting off a sky-rocket 'overexuberant'? I joined Hados with the score at 2 for 67 and together we forged a third-wicket partnership of 150 runs. Quite a few commentators watching the match felt that the big Queenslander self-ishly hogged a bit of the strike, but of course, that's not for me to say.* When I did get to face a ball everything seemed to come together for me. The footwork was right, stroke placement spot-on and by the luncheon interval I was seeing the ball like a footy. But just when another century beckoned disaster struck and I was given out lbw despite being so far forward I was practically rubbing up against the umpire. (A physical act Mr AV Jayaprakash would no doubt enjoy.) Fortunately, Tugga and Hados managed to see out play with their wickets intact and we reached stumps on a very healthy 3 for 326.

I tell you what, there's nothing like a 'good day at the office' to lift team morale and this evening we all went out in search of a good feed and a few laughs. Unfortunately, entertainment options are pretty limited here in Chennai where

* Although he clearly did.

A great day in the field marred a few moments after this shot was taken when Tugga attempted to go through the gate ahead of me despite having scored 27 fewer runs. We didn't speak for over a year.

watching each other receive physio treatment constitutes a big night out, but we eventually found a decent bar and spent a few hours relaxing together. My good mood was quickly shattered, however, upon arriving back at the hotel to find a faxed copy of an interview Ros had done for some women's magazine back in Australia. We'd signed this deal last year where all we had to do was provide them with four stories a year, crap like 'Ros and Warwick's Cricket Love Nest', but I never agreed to Ros doing an actual interview. And certainly not of such a personal nature. Reading the article I could only assume she must have been pissed. Let me take this opportunity here and now to state categorically that I have *never* 'made love while watching a Pura Cup match'. A one-day international, maybe, but never a domestic fixture.

Monday March 19

Australia vs India
3rd Test, Chidambaram Stadium, Day 2

The way of the Warrior is not the will to fight
But fighting the will . . .
(Chinese philosopher Sun Tzu, read by
John Buchanan before play, Day 2)

Today did not begin well for us. Things turned bad in the sixth over when Tugga became one of the few batsmen in history to be given out, handled ball. According to our skipper he was still confused by Buck's pre-match poem and after attempting a sweep shot he instinctively went to push the ball away. Naturally the Indians, who wouldn't know the meaning of sportsmanship if it bit 'em on the arse, appealed loudly and Tugga was on his way for 47. His wicket sparked a collapse, with Punter, Warney, Dizzy and Funky all going for ducks while the best Gilly could manage was 1. Hados was the last man out, with a magnificent 203 next to his name. Chief destroyer for the home side was Harbhajan Singh who took seven wickets. Not bad for a bloke who only has two balls — an off-spinner and one that comes straight on.

Any hopes that the Indians might also collapse quickly faded when Das and Ramesh got off to a flying start. Our bowling attack was slightly depleted when Pigeon was forced to leave the ground with the runs. There's no doubting this country takes its toll on tourists, whether it's the heat, the noise or the dodgy food. But that said, every day in India also throws up a surprise, a sight rarely ever seen. Today it was the sight of Warney taking a wicket. With Ramesh gone for 61, Laxman joined Das to take the score on to 211 in the final over of the day. By this stage Pigeon was back on and he and Dizzy were operating at full tilt, trying desperately for one last wicket before the close of play. Despite his huge knock in the second Test Laxman was looking a little shaky, especially against the short stuff, and it's in situations like this that a few 'mind games' can be very valuable. With just one ball remaining Tugga made a few fielding adjustments, moving a couple of slips into place for an edge and close-in fieldsmen onto either side. Of course there was plenty of encouragement from the lads for Pigeon to test out the centre of the pitch and we hoped that by this stage the thought of a short-pitched delivery would be well and truly

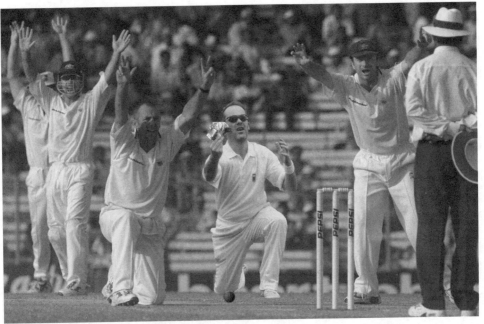

The Indian umpires refuse yet another vigorous appeal.

entrenched in Laxman's mind. To complete the scheme at the last moment Tugga moved mid-on to leg gully and fine leg to leg slip, ensuring that the batsman would be expecting nothing but a searing bouncer. At which point Pigeon came in and bowled one. Not surprisingly, Laxman survived and the Indians went to stumps on 1 for 211 in pursuit of our 391.

After a tough day in the field it felt good getting back to our rooms and relaxing in a warm bath. I've gotta say, things have improved here in India quite a bit over the years, especially in terms of hotel accommodation. When I think back to my first youth tour here in '85, we were staying in grotty, overcrowded hostels with a lot of guys sleeping two to a bed. Although, to be fair to our hosts, in some cases this was a lifestyle decision (and I'm pleased to say that none of them made it to Test level).

Tuesday March 20

Australia vs India
3rd Test, Chidambaram Stadium, Day 3

The Indians are batting well, we're almost out of luck,
Slats and Gilly failed again, Punter's made a duck,
Warney's flipper's failed him, Pigeon's on the can,
It's just the price you pay for making me 12th man.

(Damien Martyn, read before play, Day 3)

A nice surprise greeted me this morning, a letter from the Prime Minister of Australia. Everyone knows John Howard is a real cricket buff and no doubt our leader has been closely following my progress on tour so far and felt like dropping me a line. Turned out to be a pamphlet announcing changes to the GST.

It was hard to judge the team mood at breakfast. Punter's obviously a little down, having notched up scores so far of 0-0-6-0 and 0. As I quipped to him at the buffet, 'That's not a scorecard, it's the international dialling code!' This remark was taken in good humour, eventually, and once the glass fragments from the coffee jug were removed from my head we all headed for the ground determined to knock the home team over as quickly as possible.

Das and Laxman both went early, bringing Ganguly to the wicket who was caught on 22. He was surprised by a smart ball from Pigeon who put one in short, causing the Indian skipper to pop a catch up to Punter in the gully. It was called out but Ganguly stood his ground, gesturing to the square leg umpire and pointing to his shoulder to indicate it should have been called a no-ball as it was over shoulder height. (Impossible, given it hit an arsehole.) The cocky little prick eventually shuffled off, leaving Tendulkar to notch up another big century. I tell you what, there's nothing more sapping than standing in the hot sun watching your pace brigade get belted all over the park. I always believe in backing up our bowlers wherever possible and today I must have called out 'bowled mate' at least 400 times, including seventeen calls in the one over. Just when the Indians were looking set for a monumental score Dizzy and Funky stepped in to take 5 late wickets, limiting the home team to 9 for 480 at stumps, a lead of just 89 runs. For me the day was marred only by the wicket of Dravid who slashed at a wide delivery from Dizzy and edged the ball towards me at third slip. I dived forward and just managed to take the catch, only to find Dravid standing his ground. There was no doubt in my mind the catch was legitimate and for this bloke to stand there defiantly was as good as calling me, Warwick Todd, a cheat. Fortunately commonsense prevailed and the umpire's finger went up, followed by mine as I directed the little shit back to the rooms. Of course, up in the commentary box replays were being shown with a number of 'experts' insisting they could see the ball hitting the ground and so by the time I went down to field on the boundary the crowd was quite hostile. At one point after fielding a ball I was actually booed which, I can tell you, is not a pleasant sensation. In fact, I've only ever been booed once before in my life and that wasn't even on a cricket field, it was during my wedding speech when I made a distasteful joke about Ros's sister Gwen who I now admit is not, and never was, a lesbian.

Wednesday March 21

Australia vs India
3rd Test, Chidambaram Stadium, Day 4

Aussie, Aussie, Aussie,
Oi, Oi, Oi . . .

(Glenn McGrath, read for him before play, Day 4)

Gilly, Funky and Buck all lodged official reports after receiving suspicious phone calls this morning. They are concerned it could have been bookies seeking to influence the outcome of the match, although how Buck could possibly do this remains a mystery. Cut his post-match analysis back to just half an hour? Misquote a Chinese philosopher?

It didn't take long after play began for us to pick up the final wicket, ending India's innings on 501, a lead of just 110. Tugga's speech before we commenced our second innings was short and to the point: 'Good luck and no sweeping.' Hados was the first to go, out for 35 sweeping a ball from Kulkarni that flew to deep mid-wicket. With Hados out Tugga decided to regain the initiative by promoting our explosive keeper Gilly to first drop in order to shake things up a little and give him time at the crease. Hopefully the eleven balls he faced were worthwhile but unfortunately his score of just 1 was not. Slats on the other hand was looking solid, batting for the first time in an ice-vest which served to not only keep him cool but prevent him from hooking. I came in with the score on 4 for 141 and got off to a good start, timing the ball nicely, but just a few overs before lunch disaster struck when I came forward to a ball from Singh, over-balanced and was adjudged stumped by the TV umpire CR Vijayaraghavan. I'm not sure what he was watching on TV at the time but it couldn't have been the same game because I clearly managed to get my left foot back behind the crease. I'm

Harbhajan Singh wears the baggy black with pride.

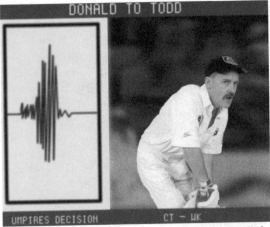

The alleged 'noise' was simply me passing wind in relief.

all for technology helping to improve umpiring decisions but in many cases I think it can be a real double-edged sword. Channel 9 'experts' once declared me out caught behind after their much-vaunted 'snickometer' registered a noise as the ball passed my bat. What this whiz-bang technology failed to indicate was that the noise was me breaking wind in relief that the ball had missed my bat. Footage of today's stumping was pretty inconclusive and I really feel I should have been given the benefit of the doubt. Of course, things weren't helped by excitable Indian keeper Dighe claiming the wicket despite clearly seeing I was back behind the line. Now don't get me wrong, I'm not calling him a cheat (although he is one) but it was a pretty unsportsmanlike display. After lunch Junior knocked up a fine half century before falling victim to Singh, which brought the hideously out-of-form Punter to the crease. The talented young Taswegian was dropped behind before he'd even scored, then dropped from a caught and bowled in the very next over. It was the best start he's had in weeks. Unfortunately it didn't last long, just 11 runs, and with Warney out off the last ball of the day we went to stumps on 7 for 241, a slender lead of just 131.

Thursday March 22

Australia vs India
3rd Test, Chidambaram Stadium, Day 5

We might be on our knees,
With our backs against the wall,
But we'll wear the baggy green with pride
And stand up straight and tall.
Focus on the match at hand,
Not go down without a fight,
Let's all be the man today
Post-match drinks, 6.30 tonight . . .

(Steve Waugh, read before play, Day 5)

Well, we lost. Despite a gallant effort from all the boys, India simply outplayed us. Looking back on today's match perhaps the words I most remember came from our vice-captain Gilly who gathered everyone round him and said, 'Faced with defeat the best thing to do is simply accept it, put it behind you and look towards tomorrow.' Good advice, for sure, but perhaps a tad premature as he was speaking during the first drinks break. Mind you, things hadn't gone all that well up until then. We'd started the day with a lead of 131 and the plan was to extend this to around 200. Unfortunately, we only got as far as 264, a lead of just 154 which was always going to be difficult to defend. Things weren't exactly made easy for us by the negative tactics of Ganguly who had his left-arm spinner Nilesh Kulkarni bowl repeatedly outside leg stump, prompting Tugga at one point to throw out his arms in silent protest, narrowly avoiding another handled ball incident.

India got away to a good start in their second innings, reaching 2 for 101, but then Dizzy got Tendulkar and Ganguly, sparking a mini-collapse. Dravid was then out to Funky and the home team looked to be in trouble at 5 for 122, still 33 runs short. We then got Laxman after tea and they were 6 for 135, from which point they struggled to 7 for 146. With just 9 runs required and two wickets in hand the odds were still with the home team but the momentum was definitely with us. Two edged fours from stand-in keeper Dighe and a 2 from Harbhajan saw the Indians get home in a nail-biter. The two batsmen were beside themselves with excitement, jumping up and down and waving to the crowd which at least gave us the opportunity to souvenir all six stumps while they were celebrating.

Understandably, proceedings were pretty downbeat in the rooms after the match. We simply hung around for the presentations and then headed back to drown our sorrows at the hotel bar. Dizzy only made a brief appearance before returning to his room to sleep while Slats and Warney were struggling with the flu. I felt pretty dejected myself, having come over here to notch up our first series win in 32 years and been so close, only to see it slip through our hands like one of the many byes Gilly let through during the match. Not that I blame our keeper, or Warney's poor form or Punter's run of outs. When you fail to win as a Test cricketer the blame never lies with your team-mates. It lies with the umpires. I tell you what, as the evening wore on and the bottle of Johnny Walker got lower I seriously contemplated chucking it all in, walking away from the game. The constant touring, the pressures, the harsh conditions — who needs it? After fifteen years on the treadmill maybe it was time for a career change, to do something that wouldn't require me to even think about cricket ever again. I could coach Sri Lanka, or work for the Channel 9 commentary team. But then I realised it was just the bottle talking, I couldn't walk away from this game. Sport was in my blood. It was sport that originally brought Mum and Dad together; Dad was an Aussie rules player, Mum worked at a nightclub and Dad assaulted her boss during an end-of-season trip. I couldn't just walk away. No, I'd return to Australia and get myself back into shape for the Ashes tour. It was time to go home. Now that was something I could drink to.

April 2001

It's amazing how a few weeks away from cricket can recharge the batteries and fill you with new enthusiasm for the game. Not long ago I was seriously thinking of tossing my career in, but after returning from the Indian tour I realised that cricket was still in my blood, as well as a few other things the pathologists have not been able to identify. In addition, I had a new challenge: to regain my position in the Aussie one-day squad. I'd been left out of the one-day team for India because of a perception that I couldn't score quickly enough, but apparently a few of my explosive innings during the tour matches had caught the eye of the selectors. It was just a question of keeping fit and waiting. In the meantime I had plenty to keep me busy, what with training, publicity and writing anonymous letters about myself to the Australian selectors. During this time I was approached by the *Herald-Sun* in Melbourne to write a kid's cricket column. Unfortunately it was axed after just one edition.

Dear Toddy,
I am in Year 7 and often try out for my school's cricket team but rarely get picked to play because I am not very good at batting or bowling. However, I do enjoy the game. Should I persist?
– Simon, Brisbane

Dear Simon,
I've met blokes like you before and quite frankly you're a waste of practice facilities. If you can't make the grade at this age you never will and would be better off playing another sport like table tennis or maths.

Dear Toddy,
I have often dreamed of one day playing cricket for Australia but wonder what is it really like?
– Brandon, ACT

Dear Brandon,
If you ask me, playing for Australia is a top job. Where else can you get paid to travel the world with a top bunch of blokes, fight hard during the day and get pissed every night? The Australian navy I guess, but the food's shithouse and you might sink.

Dear Toddy,
I've read about binge drinking being a major problem for a lot of our young sports stars and wondered if you had any thoughts on how we might tackle this serious issue?
– Hugh, ACT

Dear Hugh,
Get stuffed.

Friday April 13 was the day scheduled for the Ashes squad to be announced and most of us hopefuls sat at home all morning hoping our phones would remain silent. Standard selection practice is that those who have been left out get called by selectors before the team is announced. Of course, most of the guys like to ring each other just for a stir and at 10.50 am. I put a call through to Junior who had a good laugh when he realised it was me. I then rang Slats who threatened to come round and kill me. The good news was that I not only made the Test squad but also the one-day team, which means I'll be heading off in a little over a month. As usual there were a couple of blokes unlucky to miss out; guys like Blewie and Jamie Cox. And, as always, the unluckiest spinner in the world, Stuey McGill. But my advice to him is to simply remain patient. It can't be long before Warney retires, is injured or gets arrested.

The next few weeks were spent in a flurry of packing, training and chasing down sponsors. In late April the ICC's anti-graft chief Paul Condon made public his report on corruption in the game. Even though I was not specifically charged with any wrongdoings in the report, I felt that featuring my face on the front cover might have created a negative impression.

It was certainly a wide-ranging report and numerous players were investigated, including:

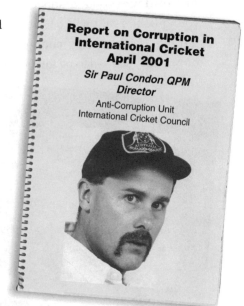

- Ranatunga and Aravinda de Silva (Sri Lanka)
- Alec Stewart (England)
- Martin Crowe (New Zealand)
- Warwick Todd (Australia)
- and anyone who's ever played for (Pakistan)

One of the more interesting recommendations of the report was that players should have their access to mobile phones restricted. Fine in theory, but a lot of us have sponsorship deals with Ericsson or Nokia. Of the ten Test-playing countries, only two were not implicated in corruption allegations — Zimbabwe and Bangladesh. Mind you, who in their right mind would *pay* a Zimbabwean or Bangladeshi batsman to play badly?

Saturday May 26

I tell you what, after 15 years of touring life, saying goodbye doesn't get any easier, especially at the start of such a long trip. When I last got back from the Ashes tour in '97 it felt like so much had changed at home — including most of the locks. That was a rocky period for my marriage to Ros, not helped by the British press making outrageous allegations about my personal affairs in just about every daily news-paper. Honestly, it was a vendetta. I'd only have to be photographed next to a woman in the pub and the tabloid sleaze merchants would beat up a story about our 'relationship' under the headline 'Wozza's Wicked Ways!' You can imagine how Ros felt reading this crap back in Australia and half my spare time was spent on the phone trying to reassure her the gossip was all complete rubbish. The other half was spent chatting to women in pubs but that's just the pressure of touring life. At least my two daughters are now older. A lot of the guys are leaving behind young babies and will be missing out on three months of sleepless nights, early morning feeds, nappy changing and toddler tantrums. Looking around at the airport they seemed to be taking it surprisingly well. The only person really struggling with separation pain seemed to be Slats who was openly crying as he kissed his loved one goodbye. He's barely had that Ferrari for six weeks and clearly parting with it was not easy for the big opener.

There's no denying the fact that departure is an exciting time but it's also one tinged with a touch of apprehension. What if I fail at the crease? What if I'm injured? What if that immigration officer spots the fifty packs of duty-free Winfields I tucked inside Hados's hand luggage? No point worrying about it I guess and at 3.30 pm the call finally came to board our flight to Singapore. An interesting feature of the pre-flight safety talk these days is a warning about the dangers of deep vein thrombosis or DVT. This

Magilla didn't take the news of his omission from the Ashes squad all that well . . .

condition can be a very real problem for the touring cricketer and occurs after long periods of inactivity such as sitting on a plane or fielding at fine leg. Fortunately no one suffered an attack on this trip and eight incident-free* hours later we landed in Singapore.

* There was one minor 'incident' that took place shortly before we touched down. Singapore has special quarantine rules where they spray disinfectant down the aisles of the plane before anyone gets off. This time however, it wasn't quarantine officials doing the spraying but a certain middle-order batsman with two cans of Brut and a hostie's jacket on. You can imagine the overpowering smell of Brut deodorant and people coughing and choking, yet somehow the cabin crew failed to see the lighter side of the incident. Perhaps they were still pissed off by an earlier incident in which I'd been fumbling around beneath my seat for a magazine and inadvertently inflated the emergency life-raft. Twice.

Sunday May 27

The stop-over in Singapore was mercifully brief, just enough time for the smokers in the squad to light up and all of us to enjoy a few cleansing ales in the transit bar. We were soon airborne again en route to Dubai, but to be honest I don't remember much about the trip as I appeared to have been seated away from the other guys and simply must have dozed off shortly after dinner. The next thing I recall was the captain announcing that we had landed — in Los Angeles.

Making the most of our brief stop-over.

Monday May 28

A quick connecting flight later I eventually managed to catch up with the boys at Attaturk Airport in Istanbul for a very special stop-over visit to the Gallipoli peninsula. I tell you what, I thought I knew what it meant to be an Aussie but this trip changed that forever. It was a beautiful spring day as we walked the beaches and famous cliffs, guided by a retired Turkish naval captain, Ali Efe. Memories of this day will remain etched in my mind forever. We saw Hell Spit and another famous beach, I can't quite remember its name, and so many graves. I was a little disappointed we didn't get to see the Kokoda Trail but obviously there was not enough time to take in everything. It was an awesome feeling, standing in trenches at the Nek, imagining those Aussie soldiers going over the top knowing they didn't have a hope. All these years later it's hard even to think what that would have been like. Scotland vs South Africa in the '99 World Cup perhaps.

Being there I realised clearly that I, Warwick Todd, am just a cricketer and that my actions on the field will not change the world, but I also felt inspired by the bravery of these soldiers before us and I hope to draw on that Anzac spirit when we get to England. Funny, we're often called 'heroes' and I guess in some ways we are, but there's no doubting the blokes who gave up their lives in this place are the real heroes. Honestly, you wouldn't believe the devastation we witnessed. According to Ali the Aussie soldiers barely advanced one kilometre in eight weeks. They were the most hopelessly under-manned, out-gunned and doomed squad of Aussies ever to do battle abroad, matched only perhaps by Graham Yallop's Ashes squad of 1979.

A special part of the visit involved us re-enacting that famous match played here on December 15 when the Anzac diggers staged a game of cricket to distract the Turkish forces while their comrades went about a mass evacuation. The 'pitch'

wasn't much to get excited about as it was covered in waist-high gorse, but this didn't stop the boys splitting into two teams and starting play. It was a truly poignant moment for us all, marred only by Punter disputing an lbw decision and threatening to ram his bat up Pigeon's arse if he didn't withdraw the appeal. Dizzy and Bev then got involved, calling our team 'a pack of lying cheats' at which point things turned really ugly. Ali later remarked they hadn't seen such fierce fighting here since 1915.

Tuesday May 29

After a morning of sightseeing around the Blue Mosque and rambling Grand Bazaar it was back onto the plane for the final leg of our epic journey to the UK. All up, from Sydney to London, I think we've spent 29 hours in the air (counting the extra three spent circling Heathrow after Tugga's mobile went off on final approach and jammed the plane's navigation systems). But in that time we've had a chance to get to know each other and bond as a group and I'm convinced this squad is as good as any I've played with, making us hot favourites to win. This said, I still got Ros to put two grand on a series loss at National Sportsbet before we left, just in case the wheels fall off. That way it's a win — win situation.

As is usual there was a huge mob of press photographers and journalists waiting to meet us at Heathrow airport; a reminder of the constant pressure and scrutiny we shall be under for the next few months. No one knows this more than our champion blonde leggie. I remember when the Aussie team arrived in the West Indies for the 1999 tour. Warney stepped off the plane after 72 hours of travel with his tie loosened. So fierce was the media scrutiny that the photos of him were instantly sent round the world, a blessing in disguise for me as I was stumbling off the plane behind him at the time without any pants.

Our first official duty after clearing customs was the traditional media conference in front of every cricket-related journalist in the land. This used to be a truly daunting experience, especially for the younger blokes, but now every team member is prepared for the Q&A session thanks to an intensive media training class conducted by the ACB before we left. Which makes it all the more surprising that within the space of half an hour I managed to call Nasser Hussain a 'B-grade slogger', Chris Atherton a 'washed-up hack' and the Queen Mother 'a drunken old fart', before media manager Brian Murgatroyd succeeded in getting the microphone out of my hand. It was the jet-lag.

It was late in the afternoon when we boarded the team bus for the trip down to Worcester where the hotel staff put on a small cocktail party to welcome us. It was a nice gesture, spoilt only by the fact they insisted on being there too. Two hours stuck in conversation with an assistant-housekeeper and I was ready for bed.

It must have been jet-lag.

Wednesday May 30

I woke around 7.00 am to a typically cold and damp English morning. Turned out I'd fallen asleep in the shower, thanks no doubt to a few too many welcoming cocktails. There was great amusement at breakfast over the front page of the *Daily Mirror*, which featured the heads of Tugga, Warney and Pigeon on the bodies of three prawns with the headline, 'Let's Throw a Few Prawns on the Barbie and Watch England Clean Up the Ashes'. Tugga and Pigeon thought it was hilarious, but Warney was immediately on the phone to his manager exploring the possibility of stitching up a sponsorship deal with a seafood company.

There's been a fair bit of focus in the press over here on the average age of our squad which apparently exceeds 30 for the first time in half a century. The way some journos are describing us you'd think we were a bunch of doddery old-aged pensioners!

A relaxed morning training session at the local ground was attended by all of us except Junior and Pigeon, who are battling a bit of gout, and it gave us the opportunity to dust off the cobwebs before returning to the hotel for lunch and our first full team tour meeting. Our manager Steve 'Brute' Bernard kicked things off by reminding us all that over here we are ambassadors for our country, a role that brings with it huge responsibility. On the positive side though, it also technically makes us immune from prosecution. But the main topic of discussion was the possibility of a tour alcohol ban. During the '99 World Cup over here we all swore off the grog for the entire campaign, an approach that instilled an enormous sense of unity amongst the boys — we were all cheating and we all knew it. After much debate it was finally agreed that we would implement an alcohol ban, but purely on a trial basis and that it would be reviewed a little further down the track.

The afternoon was designated free time, giving us a chance to catch up on a bit of lost sleep and do a little sightseeing. Dinner was very enjoyable, not just for the quality of food but also for the fact that we decided to lift the alcohol ban.

Thursday May 31

I tell you what, the sound of an alarm clock going off in your ear at 7.30 am is not a pleasant one. Even after a few days here in England eight hours sleep is still hard to come by due to the overheated rooms, strange surrounds and lingering effects of jet-lag. That, combined with the fact that last night's dinner didn't finish until 4.30 am. But there was no rest for the wicked and our ever eager coach Buck declared an all-day training session. Despite it officially being spring over here, it was a bitterly cold morning as we commenced our warm-up routine, consisting of a brisk 15-minute walk, followed by a one-minute run, one-minute brisk walk, 10 push-ups and 10 sit-ups. Fortunately we managed to complete most of this routine on the bus, before finally braving the cold for a final net session before tomorrow's tour match. I was happy with my form, middling the ball well despite not having so much as held a bat since March — unless you count the series of commercials I did for Herbavite multivitamins.

Incidentally, I never got paid for the ad below thanks to some do-gooder from the Australian Consumers Association who got on to the fact that a *few* of the

Hit Health Worries for Six!

With new HERBAVITE multi-vitamin capsules!

Herbavite energy range just happened to contain *small* amounts of cocaine. The next thing you know the company's gone belly up and Warwick Todd is left without so much as a cent. Worse, my name was dragged through the mud as someone who endorsed illegal drugs! Let me state here, for the record, that in 15 years of international cricket I have never taken anything stronger than an aspirin. The only exception, and one I very much regret, was during a long tour of the West Indies a few years back when I was really struggling with the heat and energy-sapping conditions. At one stage it got so bad that I almost feared falling asleep at the crease and so I asked our physio if he had anything that might keep me up. It took me two days before I realised he'd given me Viagra. And a week before I could comfortably wear a box out to bat.

Lunch was at the ground today and after an excellent roast we divided into three groups. Fitness adviser Jock Campbell conducted a series of cardio exercises, Buck put his charges through some fielding drills while Tugga supervised the rest of us who just wanted to finish dessert.

Items officially ruled out of the 'fruit' food group.

A final meeting of the entire touring party this evening saw quite a crowd gathered at the team hotel. A few people have remarked on the large number of support personnel who now accompany us, compared to a few years back when you'd be lucky to have a team manager and driver. Nowadays we've got a coach, manager, fitness trainer, media officer, physio, team historian (Steve Waugh), psychologist, scorer and feng shui consultant. And, in a first for Australian cricket, we actually have a female member of the touring party, our masseuse Rebecca Lauder. 'Bec' has been used in Adelaide for several years but up until now the boys have never been able to enjoy a decent massage away from home, unless you count those stop-overs in Hong Kong, and that's only for the single blokes. The team also enjoys the services of a full-time dietician who meets with every one of us players and discusses the things we should avoid. I mainly try to avoid these meetings, especially as they generally involve bad news, like tonight, when we received official notification that Cherry Ripes do not constitute part of the fruit food group.

Friday June 1

Australia vs Worcestershire, New Road Ground, Day 1

The New Road ground was a sell-out for the start of our three-day match against Worcestershire and the weather was predicted to be 'fine', which in England means the sleet may not be coming in horizontally. Tugga won the toss and elected to bat first. There's no doubt we were a little rusty after several months off and at one stage slumped to 6 for 178. The fall of a few Aussie wickets no doubt got the home side pretty pumped up and by the time I came in there were quite a few verbal 'pleasantries' coming from the boys in close. One comment that I was a 'stinking Aussie c*#t who should f#*k off back home' took me by surprise, not so much for its ferocity but for the fact it came from a former team-mate, Andy Bichel, who's now over here playing for Worcestershire. Whether it was Bic's welcome or just the slow, seaming wicket I struggled to really middle the ball and was lucky to make 32.

Another interesting mid-wicket exchange took place when Tugga came in to face local seamer David Leatherdale, a man he said in his last Ashes diary 'wouldn't get a bowl in a Chinese restaurant'. Leatherdale was understandably keen to make a point and, with the slip cordon calling for some 'sweet and sour', the pumped-up pie chucker actually managed to get one through and send Tugga on his way.

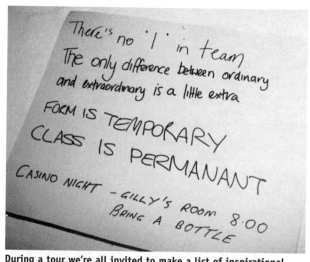

During a tour we're all invited to make a list of inspirational messages on the dressing-room wall.

I guess it's a lesson we can all learn about the danger of criticising opposition players, no matter how we feel about them, as such comments will just serve to fire up that player at some point down the track. Back in Australia I once made the mistake of calling Brian Lara a 'short-arsed has-been'. Predictably enough this comment soon got back to him — we were standing opposite each other in a pub — and the effect was immediate and frightening. Luckily security staff were able to hold him down while I shot out a back door, but it served as an important lesson.

Fortunately Marto (108) and Warney (68) combined to take our final score to 351. It would have been even higher but both blokes were dismissed lbw, despite being well forward, to left-arm spinner Matthew Rawnsley. And we thought the crap umpiring was all behind us in India! At stumps the home side was 1 for 50.

Dinner was a quiet affair and afterwards a few of us senior players went back to Tugga's room for a chat about the upcoming series. With our first one-day international against Pakistan just over a week away, Tugga, Gilly, Hados, Warney, Junior and I watched a tape of a recent encounter between them and England to try and gain an insight into their current players and form. We learnt quite a bit from the exercise, including the fact that if you spill a stubby of Foster's down the back of a VCR player a lot of smoke and blue sparks come out.

Saturday June 2

Australia vs Worcestershire, New Road Ground, Day 2

Despite their attempts to hide the fact, today was Tugga's and Junior's 36th birthday and to mark the occasion we bought them both walking sticks which were presented in the rooms before play. The catering staff also whipped up a cake for the twins but a few slices soon convinced us that the walking sticks were marginally more edible. The ground here in Worcester is so typically English — the cathedrals in the distance, the lush outfield, the manual scoreboard, the anti-Asian graffiti — it's like a scene from a film. A porn film in fact, given that play this morning was interrupted by a male streaker. At first we thought it was just our 12th man Symo trying out a new fitness routine but it turned out to be a brave, if somewhat 'underendowed',* fan.

The home side struggled to reach 163 thanks to a spirited performance from our bowling brigade, including Pigeon and Bracko with 3 wickets apiece, ably supported by yours truly who returned the figures of 4-0-63-1. Bowling is a facet of my game I really enjoy. Unfortunately, so do the batsmen and I think this may have been my last spell on tour. By stumps Australia had reached 4 for 236 with Marto and me still at the crease looking forward to some solid batting practice tomorrow.

Our tour sponsor Foster's put on a barbecue tonight that was well attended by most of the lads. Of course mad cow disease is still a bit of a worry over this way, but the general consensus was that if the chops were burnt badly enough we couldn't be in too much danger.

---

* i.e. his dick was quite small.

Sunday June 3

Australia vs Worcestershire, New Road Ground, Day 3

Marto and I came out blazing this morning and despite losing my partner for just 28 in somewhat unfortunate circumstances, I went on to post a confidence-boosting 78 not out. Marto was still sulking about the run-out when I came back into the rooms, but as I tried to explain to our *reserve* batsman, when I say 'Yes! No! Yes! No! No! Yes! No!' I quite clearly mean 'No' and he was foolish to attempt the run. Thanks to my explosive innings we reached 8 for 360 in 90 minutes, setting the home team a target of 549 off 65 overs for victory. They failed to capitalise on this sporting declaration, crumbling to be all out for just 188.

Star amongst our bowlers was Flem who took 2 wickets in 2 balls (Anurag Singh off the last ball before lunch and Graeme Hick off the first ball after lunch), only to be then denied a hat trick after his lbw shout against Vikram Solanki was turned down by our ageing excuse for an umpire. I can tell you, the big Victorian was not amused, glaring at the batsman and snatching his hat back before storming off angrily. Mind you, he does this at the end of every over. Pigeon also bowled well, taking 4 for 31, including the final wicket of tail-ender Matthew Rawnsley who he clean bowled for 0. Having played for Worcestershire last year Pigeon is a popular figure in these parts and he led the Aussie team off to a standing ovation. A few hours later very few of us were still capable of standing as we happily celebrated our first win on English soil.

Eventually we staggered out of the dressing-room and onto our team bus for the trip back to London. With all the travelling we do on an Ashes tour it's important our bus be comfortable and I'm pleased to say this year's one is very well appointed, with a TV/video, sound system, rear toilet* and even a lounge area for the card players. Such little luxuries certainly make a difference on a long tour.

Our tour bus is very well appointed.

* A few days later it was discovered that our bus did not in fact have a rear toilet, just a rear wardrobe. Fortunately a replacement vehicle was quickly found.

Monday June 4

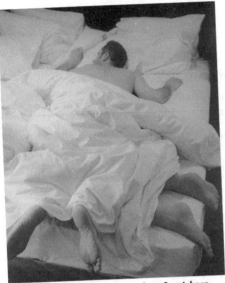

I have no idea where I am or how I got here.

To be honest I have no recollection of last night's trip down the M4 to London. All I can remember is waking up this morning in a new hotel room clutching a souvenir stump.

With a day off most of the boys opted for a sleep-in and to take care of their washing while a few of the younger blokes even shaved. I ventured outside our hotel to do a bit of shopping but soon found myself surrounded by fans all eager for an autograph and chat with an Aussie cricket star. This is the downside of fame, the way people want a piece of you, and whether it's overseas or at home I'm always being chased by someone: autograph hunters, charities, companies seeking endorsements, debt collecting agencies — the list goes on.

With another tour match due to start tomorrow a team meeting was held this afternoon. Despite our win over Worcester, Tugga believes that we are still not fully switched on and that the team's spirit is lacking 20 per cent of an indefinable quality that when it's there you don't try to think about what it is but when it's not you do. Hard to argue with. A subcommittee made up of Junior, Buck and myself has been formed to help try and identify this quality before the first one-day international next week.

We had a few drinks in the reception hall at Australia House tonight and it looked like turning into quite a pleasant evening until one of the security staff discovered we were there and threatened to call police. We then headed downtown for dinner at one of Bill Wyman's fast-food restaurants, Sticky Fingers. Bill, for anyone who's been living in a cave for the past thirty years, is a former member of the Beatles.

Tuesday June 5

Australia vs Middlesex, Lords

Still no closer to identifying the missing quality. But this didn't stop an enthusiastic Aussie team boarding the bus for the short trip to Lords. It's the first time we've been back here since defeating the Pakis in the '99 World Cup and it's good to see that repairs to much of the visitors' dressing-rooms have now been completed. There's no denying it's a special feeling to be at this ground and the chance to play in a Test match here at Lords must still represent the ultimate cricketer's dream. That, and a Nike sponsorship.

We've decided to rest Flem, Pigeon and Bev for today's match along with Gilly, giving reserve keeper Wade Seccombe the chance to launch his international career. As he has only just arrived here in England, few of us really know the guy and so I went over to him during the warm-up and said a few welcoming words. Turned out I was talking to a groundsman. I think our new blokes really should be required to wear name tags. Meanwhile there's been a late change for the home team with their captain Phil Tufnell out sick (officially flu but more likely PMT). There are rumours going round that Tuffers may be recalled for the Test squad and the selectors want to protect him from a one-day thrashing here.

The game started in perfect conditions but clouds soon rolled in and our innings went downhill like the weather. Our top order failed miserably, apart from Punter who made 57, and when I came in we were 5 wickets down with barely 100 runs on the board. It always feels good when the first ball you face hits the middle but unfortunately today it was the middle stump. Todd back in the pavilion for the dreaded duck. Luckily Harvo came to our rescue, smashing 85 off 65 balls and helping us to a final total of 232.

Lunch was of restaurant quality, as you'd expect at Lords, with the team tucking into baked cod, rack of lamb, salmon, hot pies, mousse and ice-cream. Back on the ground Middlesex got their innings off to a flying start as we struggled to break through their

It always feels good when the first ball hits the middle, but unfortunately today it was the middle stump.

93

top order. Admittedly Dizzy and Symo were unable to bowl because they were still sleeping off lunch but the home side were simply too good, knocking off the required runs in just 47 overs.

A loss by 6 wickets wasn't exactly what we hoped for this early in the tour but, as I said to the guys after the game, you must learn not to dwell on a day's events. Whether good or bad, put them behind you and move on. It's the same advice I gave Ros the day her mother died.

Back at the hotel we learnt that England was beaten today by Pakistan in the second Test at Old Trafford. Replays on the evening news showed some shocking umpiring decisions as well as pictures of Waqar Younis tampering with the ball with a thumbnail. Should be quite an interesting match next week!

Good news, our blonde pace sensation Brett Lee arrived tonight. Bad news, he's brought his guitar.

Wednesday June 6

Predictably the Pommy press have made much of our 'shock loss' yesterday to second division Middlesex, neglecting to mention the fact we'd rested half our team and were really treating the match as nothing more than a training session. Nonetheless, a lengthy team meeting was held today with the focus mainly on our match against Pakistan this Saturday. We divided into two discussion groups with the batsmen agreeing that partnerships were the key. Each time a wicket falls you lose momentum and the required run rate becomes harder to keep up with. The fast bowlers had their own meeting and according to spokesman Pigeon quite a few good ideas were discussed, but unfortunately none of the quicks could remember them.

After a short training session at Lords we made ourselves available for a media free-for-all where a lot of the focus appeared to be on the newly arrived Brett Lee. Over here Binger is seen as the archetypal Aussie — blonde, good-looking, plays in rock band — and the press were keen to speak with the big paceman. He's not actually here to play in the one-day series but has come over early to improve his match fitness. He bowled full-tilt here in the nets at Lords and team management are now trying to find him a game with a county seconds side or a league club, or failing that a couple of prison inmates willing to face a few overs in return for early release.

Big news back at the hotel with Warney announcing his sponsorship deal with Nike is now officially over. It's a sad day for our big leggie who's been with them

---

AUSTRALIAN CRICKET TEAM — TEAM RULES

1 Curfew is midnight in the hotel

2 No alcohol day before a Test

3 Curfew and drinking rules left flexible after a win (according to captain/coach)

4 Team shirt worn to all team meetings.

At the beginning of every tour team rules are drawn up. This first attempt was felt to be a little harsh and a rules subcommittee formed to come up with a few amendments.

AUSTRALIAN CRICKET TEAM — TEAM RULES

1 Curfew is midnight at any hotel

2 No alcohol hour before a Test

3 Curfew and drinking rules left flexible after a win (according to Toddy/Punter)

4 Some form of shirt worn to all team meetings.

These rules were subsequently agreed to by all.

since '94. For cricketers, losing a footwear sponsorship is a bit like a marriage ending, only more serious. It's been a tough few years for Warney on the financial front. He lost several big sponsorship deals in '98 after it was revealed he took money from illegal bookmakers and then last year that phone sex scandal led to him being dumped as Australian vice-captain. On the upside, he did score a new sponsorship deal with Vodaphone.

In a first for the tour so far, tonight did not involve a sponsor's function or charity event, giving a lot of the blokes the chance to relax or spend a bit of time in the gym. In the past touring squads would have turned any night off into a wild affair, but these days the emphasis is so much more on health and exercise. Alcohol free days (or ADFs) are an important part of the team's fitness regime and I think it's true to say most members of the squad now observe at least one a year.

Thursday June 7

Australia vs Northamptonshire

It was decided to rest three key players for today's match: Tugga, myself and Warney (who is at the Northampton day clinic having a Nike tattoo removed from his arse). With Tugga out it means our vice-captain Gilly will captain the team, a job I'm sure he'll handle adequately.

The issue of the Australian vice-captaincy has been a controversial one and I don't intend to re-open the debate here. Except to say it should have been me. Look at the facts objectively. At the end of last year the vice-captaincy was under review, with three genuine candidates for the job — Warney, Punter and yours truly. Of course, none of us had totally 'clean' records: Warney was involved in that phone sex scandal in June 2000; Punter found himself part of a Kings Cross nightclub brawl in 1999; and I backed my Mitsubishi Pajero over the foot of a Sri Lankan match referee in 1997. All unfortunate incidents to be sure, but mine took place the longest ago! It was ancient history!! Surely common sense would have suggested

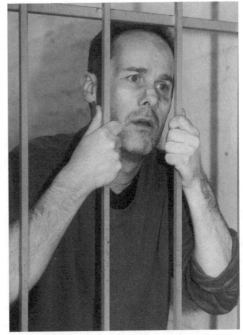

Two excellent candidates for the role of vice-captain yet each of us was overlooked.

Warwick Todd be made the next vice-captain of Australia!!! But no, the selectors opted for a 'clean-skin', the inexperienced and under-prepared Gilly, who was handed the job on a platter. Still, good luck to him.

As this was our last warm-up match before the one-day international series started, everyone was keen for a bit of time in the middle. Unfortunately our team balance was thrown out by a couple of late withdrawals: Bracko (shoulder), Punter (hip) and Junior (frostbite). It was fair dinkum freezing out on the ground with our innings interrupted three times by driving rain. Marto opened the batting and breezed to 101 not out. But our final total of 3 for 234 proved a little low as the home side steadily knocked off the required runs, just managing to reach our score in the final over.

A tied match wasn't exactly the result we were seeking but it was better than a loss and we found time to enjoy a few drinks with the Northampton boys after the game. But the festivities had to be cut short as we had a long trip ahead of us to our hotel in Wales. Most of the boys went by bus but a few of us opted for a change, completing the journey in one of the official team hire cars. Despite not playing today I was still pretty tired and keen for some shut-eye during the trip but struggled to find a comfortable position, which was probably just as well as I was driving.

Friday June 8

Another day, another predictable round of negative press, this time focusing on the fact we've been unable to beat two 'lowly placed' county teams. One of the papers also showed photos of me as 12th man yesterday *allegedly* bumping into the Northampton batsman Mike Hussey as we crossed in the player's race. As usual the story was a complete beat up. I'd just brought a new pair of glove liners out to Gilly (for the seventeenth time I might add), when this Hussey bloke emerged from the rooms. As there wasn't much space for the two of us to pass, I did the sensible thing and shoved him against the fence. Next thing I know it's being described as 'an unprovoked display of aggression'!

Shortly after breakfast a few of us bumped into our former captain, Tubby Taylor, who is over here covering the tour for Channel 9. He had heard about our failure to win the last two matches and decided to drop by the hotel to say 'hi' and share a few thoughts on what we might be doing wrong. It was very casual really, just a chat. Quite a long chat in fact. Followed by a series of one-on-one interviews. He was just in the middle of arranging a full team meeting when Tugga found out and had him removed from the premises.

Things are looking a little bleak for England at the moment, having lost yesterday's one-day series opener to Pakistan by 108 runs. To add to their woes, their one-day squad is looking in trouble. Out so far are Andy Caddick (back), captain Nasser Hussain (broken finger) and Graham Thorpe (who has apparently just cracked the shits).

At a brief team meeting we discussed our match tomorrow and the fact that even though we are officially the World Cup one-day champions we must not be complacent and we must always respect the opposition, which won't be easy as they're Pakistanis. One interesting issue that came up was our tour motto or, more accurately, lack of one. For the past few years we've given our overseas tours a theme. In '97 the Ashes tour was summed up by the words 'Energy. Positive. Sensible' which were scrawled on every dressing-room wall and team noticeboard we used. Some of the guys even had these three words tattooed on their butts. A practice that ended abruptly when the '99 World Cup motto was declared 'Every Sacrifice We Make is a Down Payment on the Acquisition of the World Cup' — you'd need an arse bigger than the Duchess of York's to fit that one on. A search for this year's motto is now under way with a subcommittee established to consider suggestions.

Saturday June 9

Aust vs Pakistan
1st One-Day International, Millennium Stadium

Well, this is it — the start of our international campaign. I was up early for breakfast: bacon and eggs, hash browns, French toast and pancakes washed down with a cup of hot coffee (reduced-fat milk naturally). The new Millennium Stadium here in Cardiff has a roof so being rained on will not be a problem. But getting spat upon by the volatile Paki crowd of 11 000 could well be. I don't think there's anything more grating than the sound of Pakistani cricket fans blowing noisy, tuneless trumpets, unless it's the sound of Tugga's warm-up music this morning — an awful John Williamson song about bloody galahs or something.

The boys were a little toey, keen to get through the pre-match warm-ups and onto the field. Warney was taking no chances and out of his kit bag came the famous lucky creams in which he once took 8 for 71. Unfortunately they were now full of lucky holes, courtesy of star prankster Bev and a pair of scissors. I don't think our big leggie saw the funny side but the rest of us enjoyed a laugh.

A couple of last-minute withdrawals from the side (Hados, Flem and Bracko) saw Brett Lee make a surprise appearance in the team. There's no doubting Bing's come-back to international cricket has been an absolute marvel when you consider all that he has been through. It was just over a year ago that the powerful paceman was reported by a couple of Indian umpires for chucking during a Test against New Zealand. He then had some tests which showed his arm was in fact permanently bent (a condition very familiar to many Indian umpires), which turned out to be the result of an injury sustained during an Australian under-17 carnival in Tassie when a beer keg rolled on top of it. No sooner had Binger been cleared of chucking than the big fella was then forced to have an operation on his shoulder to correct a stress-related injury caused not by his bowling action, but by his aggressive method of appealing. It's great to see that now after so much guts and hard work he's back in the side.

The Pakis batted first and to celebrate his return Bing had Shahid Afridi brilliantly caught at second slip by Junior in his first over. But after that the big paceman really got belted around, having 85 runs taken off his 10 overs. Warney took a wicket with his first ball, a ripping leg break that beat Abdur Razzaq. It almost beat Gilly too but he eventually managed to grab the ball and effect a stumping. Three balls

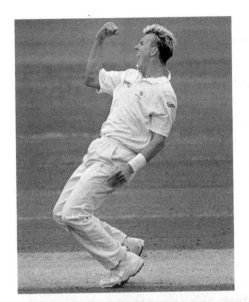

At first it was thought Lee's injuries were caused by his bowling action . . . but his technique of appealing placed far greater stress on his body.

later Warney had form batsman Inzamam-ul-Haq stumped for a duck. Ul-Haq practically danced down the wicket, swinging wildly at the ball, a very strange move from such a fine player. Of course I'm not suggesting for a second that there was anything suspect about this and that he might have been deliberately throwing his wicket away in return for a considerable cash payment organised through a Bombay betting syndicate some days prior to the match. Such a suggestion would be completely ridiculous, as I later said in the small note I dropped to Sir Paul Condon. However, it was a little odd when the Pakistan batsman joined in his own post-wicket celebrations. Anyway, after 25 overs the Pakis had crashed to 6 for 88, but then they hit back with Yousuf Youhana belting 91* and Rashid Latif 66 to create a total of 257.

If Binger's inclusion caught the Pakis by surprise they had their revenge with the last-minute selection of Shoaib Akhtar. He was immediately back to his fiery best, sending down a succession of missiles at the Aussie batsmen. To make matters worse, the white Duke balls they use over here in England tend to be harder and smaller than the Australian Kookaburra balls which, as a negative, causes them to dart around a little more. (As a positive it provides me with a great opening joke for one of my sportsmen's night routines). But we weathered the pace storm and picked off the required runs without any real problem with Junior, Punter, Bev and Tugga all sharing the credit. I was clean bowled on 13 by Akhtar from a delivery that the TV replays clearly showed to have been a no-ball. This sort of shoddy umpiring is a blight on the game, and I wasn't surprised to hear quite a few irate calls to BBC radio after the match complaining about the unfairness of my dismissal. It was good of Warney to lend me his mobile.

It was great opening our one-day account with a convincing win and naturally a few quiet drinks were enjoyed in the rooms after play as we were able to sit back and relive highlights of the match. Binger's figures of 1 for 85 turned out to be an Australian one-day record, beating Pigeon's previous worst of 1 for 76 against Sri Lanka five years ago. We reminded both of them about these bowling spells and the two boys enjoyed a good laugh. Eventually. Interestingly, Akhtar clocked the fastest delivery of the day, breaking Lee's record with a 156.3 km/h bullet. He certainly was coming in quick today and personally I don't think I've seen anything moving towards me quite that fast since our training camp last January when I was standing in the carpark and Slats drove up late for a net session.

Sunday June 10

Australia vs England
2nd One-Day International, Bristol County Ground

We arrived here in Bristol early last night and continued the celebrations in style at the hotel bar,
unaware that several local press photographers
were lurking in the shadows. Consequently, a few
of the lads woke this morning to see pictures of
themselves enjoying a 'chat' with several female
fans, pictures that will no doubt find their way
into Australian newspapers in the coming days.
It's an occupational hazard for blokes with girlfriends or partners back home,
women who don't always understand the pressures and loneliness that come with
a long overseas campaign. Back on the '93 Ashes tour Ros was furious when I was
snapped chatting with a young blonde fan in a cocktail bar. The 'pressures and
loneliness' argument didn't hold a lot of weight back then as the shot was taken at
Sydney airport before we'd even left, but I still gave it a go.

Another big one-day crowd greeted us when play
began at the county ground. The major positive about
today was I got to spend some much needed quality
time out in the middle. The negative — it was as 12th
man, carrying new gloves and drinks to those show-
ponies Punter and Marto. England won the toss and
batted first, struggling to make just 25 runs off the first
10 overs. Then Knight and Trescothick really took it up
to us, belting our bowlers all over the park until Knight
holed out for 84, caught off a quicker delivery from
Lee that TV replays apparently showed was a no-ball.
Frankly I think these sorts of replays are an unneces-
sary part of the game and if the umpire fails to spot a
problem then that's just the luck of the draw.

The Poms ended up with a total of 4 for 268, a reasonable target that would take a bit of chasing. Our
batsmen slipped into gear well, with Junior, Marto and

**The major positive about today is I
got to spend some much needed time
out in the middle. The negative —
it was as 12th man.**

Punter all making good starts. But despite this, towards the end the required run rate had crept up to 8 an over, and with 11 runs needed off the last 7 balls the equation was looking a little tight. As you could imagine, there was a fair bit of tension in the rooms, partly because of the tight finish, but more due to the fact that Junior had a sure thing going round in the fourth leg at Epsom Downs. Out in the centre Ben Hollioake was really tying Tugga and Harvo down when the latter smacked a big 6 to really take the pressure off. England was then forced to bring its field in, allowing Tugga to hit another two boundaries and win the match with 3 balls to spare. Junior's horse came fifth.

The Man of the Match cheque for 1500 pounds went to Punter* who was unlucky to be run out on 102 when Symo turned his back as the talented Taswegian set off for a second run. These sorts of mid-wicket mix-ups can often lead to ill feeling between players and it was good to see after the match that there was no friction between the two team-mates. In fact, there was no contact between them at all, Punter having locked Symo out of the rooms at the close of play.

England are now firmly at the bottom of the triangular one-day table with acting captain Alec Stewart acknowledging that they are 'third favourites'. After today's performance they may have slipped to fourth.

As we were leaving the ground this evening an Aussie fan approached me with the ball Tugga had hit to the boundary to score our winning runs. This kind-hearted cobber had managed to retrieve the prized cherry and offered it to me on condition I mention his name in this book. Sorry mate.

* The cheque actually goes into the team prize pool, to be used for social activities, paying for structural damage to hotels and dressing-rooms and posting bail.

Monday June 11

Another cold, wet day greeted us here in Bristol this morning with the team offered a choice of activity: training or a guided tour of former England wicket-keeper Jack Russell's art gallery. I don't think I've ever seen such a solid turnout to one of Jock Campbell's fitness sessions.

After lunch we boarded the team bus for Manchester where yet another official team function awaited; a dreary dinner put on by the England and Wales County Cricket Board. These are considered hard work by most of the lads as we are generally split up, one to a table, and required to entertain a circle of elderly English cricket fans. Honestly, you sit there for half an hour being asked predictable questions like, 'So, how do you think you Aussies will do then?' by some ancient twit who then wanders off, only to be replaced by another equally ancient twit who asks exactly the same questions. The only relief is being able to sneak out to the dunnies for a smoke every so often where you can at least catch up with the other boys. At one stage tonight there were 14 members of the Aussie squad taking a leak simultaneously and complaining about how bored they were. The only non-Aussie there was an elderly ECCB member who explained that he too was bored out of his brain. Apparently he'd been seated next to Buck.

∾ Official ECCB Dinner ∾

6.00	Welcoming drinks
6.20	Official welcome by team manager
6.30	Drinks
6.45	Pre-dinner drinks
7.00	Entree served (including drinks)
7.30	Official toast
7.40	Team responds to official toast
8.00	Main course served (with drinks)
9.00	Dessert served (includes dessert wines)
9.30	After-dinner drinks
11.00	Return to hotel
11.15	Drinks

❖

Tuesday June 12

Another typical English day here in Manchester, cold, damp and gloomy. Outside the hotel it wasn't much better as we headed off to training. I put in a good session, playing straight and really watching the ball which left me feeling confident, so much so that I opted for a second net session against some local second XI bowlers. One of them, a gangly-looking teenager with blue hair and a nose-ring, managed to clean bowl me twice, shattering my new-found confidence in just a few overs. This will teach me the dangers of over-training.

During lunch my work commitments continued as I prepared to interview a few of the boys as part of my affiliation with Channel 10. I was just after some comments about the one-day series but ran into trouble finding anyone officially allowed to talk on camera. Half the guys are tied up exclusively with Channel 9 and the rest have contracts with Channel 7 or Foxtel, meaning the only decent interview I could

We've made a conscious effort to improve on-field behaviour.

get was with Buck. I asked our coach a simple question about the upcoming match against England and by the time my cameraman indicated that his 45-minute video tape had run out, Buck was still going strong. I just hope they can edit something out of it.

Our hotel is not far from the Manchester United soccer grounds and after an extensive net session Tugga, Gilly, Hados and I took a tour of the famous club's facilities before heading back for a lengthy team meeting during which we agreed to target a few of England's key players. Their opener, Marcus Trescothick, is looking dangerous so far and we considered the best way of getting him out could be a short ball down leg side that he might be tempted to flick through to the keeper. Psychologically, it's always good to knock over a team's captain and we felt that taking Alec Stewart's wicket could just be a matter of putting the ball in 'the corridor of uncertainty', which in his case these days tends to be anywhere in front of the wicket. In terms of on-field behaviour, we've made a conscious decision this tour to clean up umpire dissent and Tugga said that from now on he wanted us to accept all decisions, even if we don't agree with them. He kept looking in my direction while he was saying this, which I felt was a little pointed.

I gave Ros a ring tonight, just to see how she was coping back home. It's not easy managing on your own with two young kids but at least things are a little easier for her now that the girls are older. I remember when our first daughter Raleisha-May was born, it really put a lot of pressure on our relationship. Ros was constantly tired and she struggled with the housework and cooking, as well as in the 'bedroom department'. At one point Ros suggested we get a maid in, but I said to her, 'I don't feel comfortable sleeping with a maid', at which point she became all irrational and locked me out of the house.

Wednesday June 13

If we thought our fitness guru Jock Campbell would go easy on us this morning we were very wrong and at 9.30 am the team found itself out on the field in the middle of an exhausting training session. The one plus is Jock's fresh approach to fitness and instead of the regulation running and stretching, we've often found ourselves playing volleyball, touch footy, even Totem tennis. Naturally these unorthodox methods attract a fair share of derision from onlookers, and today was no exception as we completed a hard-fought round of off-ground chasey followed by a 22-metre egg-and-spoon race.

Our fitness workout was followed by a net session and with the next match scheduled for tomorrow it was noticeable that everyone had stepped up a notch in intensity. Of course this can lead to problems as our fast bowlers strive for that extra yard of pace, and it wasn't long before Bev copped a nasty blow to the thigh, chucking his bat away in a typical display known to us all as a case of the 'Bevattacks'. Today's outburst from the nuggetty New South Welshman was quite mild compared to earlier incidents. I remember once seeing him hit on the finger in the nets. He not only chucked his bat away but walked up, grabbed the bowler responsible by the collar and threatened to 'punch the shit' out of him. The poor kid was barely 12 and I believe it's the last time Bev's ever been invited to take part in a junior coaching clinic.

Tonight the entire squad went along to see a Bon Jovi concert at Huddersfield; a trip organised by Slats who is over here working as a television commentator during the one-day series. Slats is a huge fan of this band, playing them on the team CD player at just about any opportunity. In fact at Lords in '97 he was once officially reprimanded for having the volume up too high. Mind you, it was during our official meeting with the Queen.

Thursday June 14

Australia vs England
3rd One-Day International, Old Trafford

As today's match was a day–nighter we were given the luxury of a sleep-in and leisurely breakfast, but this relaxed start to the morning was rudely interrupted when we were summoned to an urgent team meeting. When I walked into the room there were a lot of grim faces and several members of management looking visibly pale. Turned out one of Tugga's John Williamson CDs had gone missing. Fortunately it was tracked down after an extensive search and not long after that we boarded the team bus.

Old Trafford is a ground that holds many memories for touring Aussie squads, and certainly for yours truly. It was here in '93 that I made a second-innings duck, walked back into the rooms and smashed up my bat so badly that later the boys all signed the broken blade and arranged to have it hung on the visitors' dressing-room wall. It hung there until 1997 when I made another duck and destroyed the wall. Hopefully my score here today will be a little higher than on those occasions!

We won the toss and elected to bat, with Hados getting his first chance in this series to convince the selectors of his credentials as a one-day opener. He lasted just four balls. To be honest, everyone struggled with the conditions as the ball darted around alarmingly and if it weren't for solid knocks from Bev, Tugga, Marto and

The visitor's viewing room at Old Trafford shortly after I made a first-ball duck.

myself we could have been in trouble. But we made it through to a semi-respectable 7 for 208 in the 48th over, at which point rain sent everyone dashing from the field.

Under the baffling Duckworth–Lewis system, England were then set a revised target of 216.35 off 44.2 overs. Tugga spoke to us during the break about 'getting in the faces' of our opponents, something our pace duo of Dizzy and Pigeon managed to do with ease, reducing the Poms to 5 for 40 in just 18 overs. Dizzy's opening spell was simply stunning, bowling Vaughan for a first-ball duck and then going on to take another two wickets. It was particularly pleasing to see him do so well after years of injuries and breakdowns that had prompted so many to write off the big South Australian as a fragile trundler, and after his third wicket I ran over and gave him a pat on the back. Unfortunately I think I may have dislocated his shoulder. Our quicks were well supported by Warney who was soon called into the attack, arriving to the usual chorus (of 'you fat bastard') coming from the usual ill-educated quarters (our own slips cordon). He took 2 valuable wickets and under this sustained assault the Poms soon slumped to be all out for 86, giving us victory by 125 runs.

It was a crushing victory, England posting its lowest one-day score ever, and we are now assured a place in the finals. Naturally there were a few celebratory ales enjoyed in the rooms after play as the lads prepared to really kick on, but it was at this point that Tugga reminded us all that we still had another match to play in two days. Sure enough, a few hours' later things had quietened down considerably, possibly because by this stage seven members of the squad had passed out.

Friday June 15

We woke to the news that there had been some controversy back home after former fast bowler turned commentator Jeff Thompson apparently dropped the f-word on TV during coverage of yesterday's match. Coming back from an ad break he commented on the lousy spring weather by saying he was 'f*#king sick of this'. I feel sorry for Thommo, having had a brief spell as a commentator myself I know the sort of pressures placed on you. During the summer of '98–99, I worked for ABC Radio as a special comments man and couldn't believe how fussy the listeners could get. The slightest mistake, like mispronouncing a batsman's name or getting the number of leg byes wrong, would cause an avalanche of complaints. People would pick you up on the smallest grammatical error, like the time I began a sentence with 'The team are' when I should have said 'The team is'. This tiny error prompted over 300 calls to the ABC switchboard. Yet the rest of the sentence ('The team are playing like a bunch of spastic girls') only prompted one person to complain. Unfortunately he was the Managing Director of the ABC and that was the end of my short-lived commentary career.

ABC Ⓐ RADIO

15 January 1999

From: The Managing Director,
       ABC Radio

To: The Head of Sport
       ABC Radio

Re: Special Comments

I wish to express my concern over several remarks made by your Special Comments man Mr Warwick Todd during the recent Test match in Melbourne. As you are no doubt aware, ABC policy expressly prohibits the broadcasting of views that may be racist, sexist, offensive or inflammatory. Mr Todd's assertion that 'These cheating Sri Lankan jungle-bunnies are the biggest bunch of girls I've ever seen pull on a skirt . . . ' managed to breach every criteria. There were also clear indications that alcohol was being consumed in the commentary box during the broadcast.

I look forward to your response.

Another cricket-related issue making the news right now is the proposed one-day series against India scheduled to be played back in Australia this November. Tugga has publicly expressed his concerns with the timing of this series as his wife is expecting their third child in that month. While I naturally sympathise with Tugga on this, I think it's a little ridiculous to suggest cancelling the series. I mean, if matches were postponed every time an Australian cricketer was due to father a child, international fixtures would be non-existent. That said, looking after your family is obviously a priority, and over the years there has been a general awareness from the ACB that some concessions must be made to ensure players get to spend time off with their loved ones when required. Recent examples include Warney being allowed to fly home from the last Ashes tour after the birth of his daughter, Pigeon missing a one-dayer because his wife was due to give birth and Punter receiving permission to leave a pre-tour training camp when one of his greyhounds was diagnosed with kennel cough.

Saturday June 16

Australia vs Pakistan
4th One-Day International, Durham County Ground

There was a near emergency this morning when, halfway to Durham, our manager Brute Bernard suddenly realised he'd left some vital pieces of team equipment back at the hotel. A quick dash back up the M2 saw our cards and crossword books hastily retrieved before setting off again for the ground. As it turned out the three-hour trip was a complete waste of time thanks to heavy rain that delayed the start of play for several hours. During the long wait for play to commence Buck and Jock attempted to organise a weights and exercise session at the ground's gym, but with the Lions–Queensland rugby match on telly, no one felt much like taking part.

Despite the Chester-le-Street groundstaff working valiantly, it was impossible to keep the pitch dry and at 2.00 pm the match was officially called off. Which was

ACB Australian Cricket Board

12 June 2001

Mr W. Todd
C/- Sportstar Management Group
PO Box 114A
BRISBANE, QLD 4001

Dear Warwick,

I am writing in regard to the recent incident at Westbury Hotel in London that has been the subject of an official Australian Cricket Board inquiry. The following findings have been reached:

We are prepared to accept your explanation that the emergency fire exit door on Floor 6 was already broken and that you had nothing to do with this damage or the ice-making machine being rolled over the mezzanine balcony railing.

We have however formed the view that you should be forced to pay for all dry cleaning expenses incurred by the concierge Mr Charles Boothby and we will be deducting the required amount from your future match payments.

Yours faithfully,

Good luck against the Pakis!

JAMES SUTHERLAND
CHIEF EXECUTIVE OFFICER

just as well really, seeing as we'd all left at 11.30. About the only action we saw all day was when new boy Nathan Bracken somehow managed to cut his finger on a door handle, an injury that required three stitches. It's probably lucky for him we didn't end up playing, otherwise he would have been featured on the injured player list as 'Bracken (knob)' which could have taken a bit of explaining. In fact, the only people really disappointed not to have played today were Flem, who is really looking for an opportunity to gain a place in the team, and Symo, who for some reason allowed Binger to give him a mohawk haircut during the long rain delay. The hair-cut, like so much of Binger's recent bowling, could at best be described as 'patchy'. Not that Symo was complaining. He was happy just to have made the one-day squad for England after suffering a freak pre-tour training accident when he fell off an esky. According to the big Queenslander, he was standing on top of the esky to reach for a suitcase when it collapsed underneath him, causing minor injuries to his shoulder. As it so happens, this was an uncanny echo of a pre-tour training accident I once suffered, only in my case it was the reverse — I was standing on top of a suitcase reaching for an esky.

Sunday June 17

We travelled to Nottingham this morning where a solid net session was scheduled at the Trent Bridge ground. Flem bowled well and there is obviously now a fair bit of competition between him, Pigeon, Dizzy and Binger for the three pace-bowling spots. Not that this was the cause of any tension or ill feeling between the boys and during the morning they could often be seen exchanging friendly words and playful punches. There was one unfortunate incident when Binger dropped a ball in a little short that nearly took Dizzy's head off. An incident made worse by the fact that Dizzy wasn't batting at the time, he was just walking past to get a drink. But this was a one-off and we completed the training session without any further in-fighting or assaults.

Back at the hotel we were shocked to hear that England had been thrashed by the Pakis at Leeds. The result itself was hardly a surprise but the events leading up to it were. Apparently the game had to be forfeited by the Poms after a pitch invasion that left one ground attendant with broken ribs. It occurred when the Pakis required just 4 runs from 10 overs, and the captain Alec Stewart was forced to concede defeat in the interests of safety as stump-stealing fans stormed the pitch. Of the pitch invaders, 90 per cent were clearly Pakistanis, although there were a small number of Pommy fans who gave themselves away after they jumped the fence and then formed an orderly queue.

With no match scheduled for tomorrow we were a little surprised this evening when Tugga and Buck called a sudden team meeting, but it sounded quite urgent and they insisted everyone be there. Turned out they were selling Amway.

Monday June 18

The hazards of touring life are many, whether it's poor food, overheated hotel rooms or, as was the case this morning, a 4.30 am fire alarm that forced every guest downstairs and into the lobby. Such a disruption the day before a big international fixture could very easily unsettle a team, but fortunately most of us were still out at a Nottingham nightclub and so avoided any major inconvenience.

The repercussions of yesterday's pitch invasion are still being felt, with ACB head honcho Mal Speed holding urgent talks today with his England and Wales Cricket Board counterpart Tim Lamb. On the agenda was a serious discussion about future ground security, but sadly their meeting had to be abandoned prematurely after several Pakistani cleaners stormed the office and tried souveniring a pen. Closer to home, Tugga gave a press conference where he repeated his concerns that if something is not done soon someone will get killed. Possibly by him. Of course he's been saying the same thing since that frightening moment in Guyana during our 1999 tour of the West Indies when 500 fans stormed the field. Since then I think the only security measure implemented by authorities is a ban on Greg Ritchie leading overseas supporters' tours. We've been promised extra security for our match tomorrow, with Nottinghamshire officials announcing plastic fencing will be rolled out with 2 wickets or 15 runs to go or if a ground invasion looks imminent. They've also introduced fines for any pitch invader not correctly attired.

On a positive note, the practice wicket here at Trent Bridge is one of the best we've seen so far in England and it would have been nice to make good use of it today but we had a golf game scheduled.

Dinner was a formal affair as team management had agreed for us to take part in a charity fund-raiser to help with some local childrens hospital. We players were forced to meet and mingle with the usual stuffy brigade while desperately

I chat with a very special fan.

trying to catch the attention of a drinks waiter whose appearances were as about as rare as Hayley's comet. But doing our bit for those in need is part and parcel of being an international cricketer and it was during this function that I met a young boy who had an enormous effect on me. His name was Declan, he was 6 years old and there with his dad, who explained that Declan suffered from a rare congenital heart condition that could end his life at any time. He did actually tell me the name of the condition but just at that moment a drinks tray went past and I was slightly distracted. Anyway, I got chatting to Declan and frankly I was pretty moved by this young bloke. I mean, here I was worrying about a minor groin strain that could, at worst, restrict my running between wickets and this kid was coping every day with a life-threatening illness. It certainly puts things in perspective and I promised Declan that my innings tomorrow would be dedicated to him.

Tuesday June 19

Australia vs Pakistan
5th One-Day International, Trent Bridge

I woke to see in the local paper a photo of me and Declan under the headline 'The Little Hero Who Stole Toddy's Heart'. God I must have been pissed last night. According to the article I've promised him a trip to bloody Disneyland. Still, it's the first piece of positive press I've received all tour.

As expected there was a big crowd down at Trent Bridge, close to 14 000. With security still a major concern our management had demanded 300 stewards be employed at the ground, a request Nottinghamshire officials responded to by hiring one steward who was aged about 300. They had at least organised for warnings about keeping off the ground to be broadcast all morning in English, Urdu and Punjabi. As well as this a short Urdu film was screened on the scoreboard featuring Pakistani players urging fans to keep off the field. However, its effectiveness as a warning was perhaps slightly limited by the fact it was done in the form of a musical.

As we have already qualified for the final it was decided to rest Pigeon, Punter and Harvo for today's match. The Pakis won the toss and batted first, making 9 for 290, with Warney and Binger both picking up two wickets. Thankfully the massive security effort prevented any ground invasions, but at one point a huge firecracker exploded near Bing who was fielding at fine leg. The big paceman admitted it was only the second time he'd ever felt threatened on a cricket field — the first being when he once dropped a catch off the bowling of Pigeon and the big man from Narromine threatened to shove a stump up his arse. After the firecracker incident Tugga immediately lead us from the field and went to speak with match referee Brian Hastings (who he found hiding in a cupboard in one of the committee rooms). Tugga made it clear we wouldn't go back on unless extra security was deployed to the trouble spots. This was eventually agreed to and we came back 17 minutes later to complete our last 5 overs.

Cricket
Bet on the Match

Match: AUSTRALIA v PAKISTAN

Winning Team or Draw: PAKISTAN   Amount: £ 50:

I deny ever making this bet.

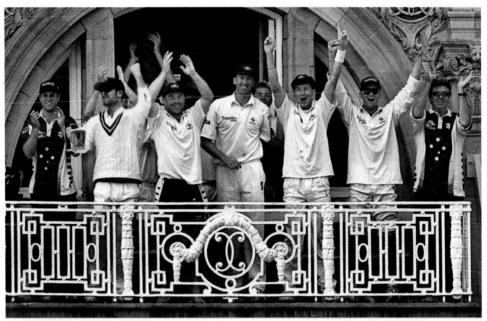

Another victory for the Aussies!

Meeting the Queen was a very special moment and one I was keen to record.

Todd Man Out

It's not hard to miss Warwick Todd, even if you're not a cricket fan. From the moment this batting legend ambles into Brisbane's Bayside Deli — a fashionable thirty-five minutes late — he exudes a certain presence.

Story **Matthew Jeffries**
Photography **Brendan Northcross**

PERHAPS it's the swagger, the gold jewellery or the constantly ringing mobile phone. Or maybe just the cloud of cigarette smoke. Whatever the reason, people immediately notice and begin pointing. Within minutes patrons are coming over, requesting autographs and photos with their hero. Todd is polite but firm in his refusal to sign anything, explaining to one fan, 'I give you an autograph and tomorrow you'll be flogging it in some pub for three hundred bucks.' As the fan in front of him is barely nine years old this claim would seem a little far-fetched, but Todd is adamant in his stance. 'Listen mate' (in our entire time together I am only ever referred to as 'mate', 'matey' and, on one occasion, 'pal') he confides, 'being recognised is part of the whole deal but there are times when you'd give anything to just blend into the furniture.' I suggest that removing his wraparound sunglasses and ACB-issue shirt might help but he dismisses the idea with a wave of his hand.

Warwick Todd, or 'Toddy' as he is known to a legion of cricket lovers the world over, is by his own admission a simple man. Just a 'bloke who likes a hit in the park and a drink with my mates'. Yet controversy has seemed to follow this Aussie icon throughout his sporting career, whether it be his frequent on-field indiscretions ('Match referees are f*#king ruining the game'), wild nightclub brawls, marital tensions or his latest, a well-publicised battle with the Australian Taxation Office. This last topic clearly gets the big left-hander fired up. 'Listen, mate, you try and do something for society, put a bit back in, you know what I mean? And these dickheads in Canberra piss all over you.' The 'dickheads' Todd refers to are, of course, federal tax inspectors who earlier this year announced a probe into the dealing of his recently registered charity Care for the Kids. The probe centred around allegations that the only children to directly benefit from the charity were, in fact, Todd's own two daughters, a claim vehemently denied by the big-hitting Test hero. 'We set aside money to help out kids in need, all kids, regardless of race, creed, colour or who they're related to. It's the f*#king tall f*#king poppie syndrome and that's for f*#king sure.'

Seeking safer territory, I switch topics to the up-coming tour of England and Toddy's thoughts on what could be his last tour of the old Dart. 'Listen mate, it's the ultimate, the pinnacle for any Test player to tour England. I just can't wait to get over there and stick it to the Poms.' At this point our conversation is interrupted by Todd's mobile phone and a very heated exchange along the lines of 'They what? Oh, for f*#k's sake, we're only asking for a footwear deal, not the complete outfit. Well tell 'em to get f*#ked or else we're going to Nike'.

Continued page 264

I was disappointed when Channel Nine pulled the plug on my 'Kid's Kricket Show' amidst claims I'd engaged in intimadatory bowling against an eleven year old.

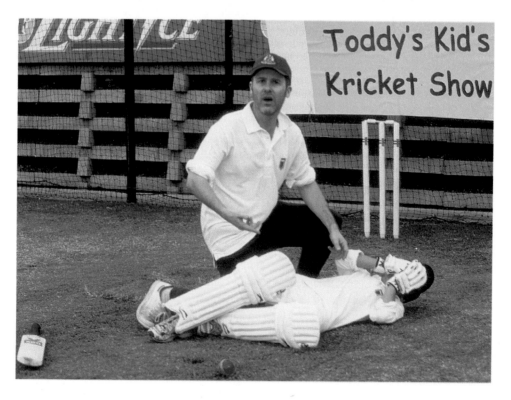

A target of 290 didn't appear all that difficult but for some reason we just couldn't put the chase together. Gilly returned to his one-day best with a fine knock of 70, but Junior and Hados both registered ducks, while Bev and Marto also went cheaply. I was conscious of having dedicated my innings to young Declan and really made an effort to get in behind every ball I faced. Both of them. I just hope the little tacker wasn't watching as I trudged off mouthing obscenities. In the end we failed by 36 runs, all out for 254 in the 46th over. It was our first loss of the tournament and afterwards there was naturally a fair bit of soul-searching, followed by searching for a pub.

Wednesday June 20

For a lot of the boys wearing sunglasses is a sponsor requirement.

Typically the Pommy press have jumped on our 'dismal' performance yesterday but to be honest none of us are all that fussed by the loss. As we explained in various interviews, it's always tough batting second under low, weak lights. Some so-called 'experts' then questioned why so many of us were wearing sunglasses but the fact is, for a lot of the guys, it's a sponsor requirement.

At the team meeting this afternoon Buck really put a rocket up us, saying we lacked commitment and discipline yesterday and that we should be ashamed of our lacklustre performance. I tell you what, our coach's comments must have hit home, with the squad instantly fired up. For the first time in quite a while it felt like we all agreed on something — that Buck not be invited to future team meetings. Tugga then threw the meeting open for suggestions on how we might improve our general on-field performances. The general consensus was that we batsmen are tightening up at the crease, trying to rush our strokes and not adapting to the slower English wickets. Our masseuse Rebecca suggested we all place a drop of bergamot oil on our collars to help combat anxiety. She may not be invited to future meetings either.

Tonight our team sponsor Travelex held a croquet tournament that was well attended by all the boys, who were attracted by the chance to learn

Despite being the only female member of our touring party, Bec joined in all our activities except for the net sessions and the farting competitions.

a new sport and the free drinks on offer. It's a very genteel pastime, croquet, with a lot of wandering around on rolling lawns gently tapping balls through hoops. Unfortunately it turned a little ugly during the second chukka when a certain middle-order batsman disputed a close decision and tossed his mallet into a pond. I'm not about to name any names here but I suspect his twin brother could be having a few stern words with him back at the hotel. In the end the match was won by Funky (who has just arrived), and Slats (who never seemed to leave).

I felt pretty bad about letting Declan down with my innings yesterday and so before turning in I rang his dad to offer them tickets to tomorrow's one-day match against England. Hopefully it will be a special day out for the brave youngster.

It was their first introduction to croquet for many of the team.

Thursday June 21

Australia vs England
6th One-Day International, The Oval

It was decided to rest Dizzy, Warney and myself for this 'dead rubber' today as part of our rotational policy. I'm not too concerned about sitting this one out as Tugga assures me it's just to give Symo a bit of time at the crease. You have to feel sorry for guys like him who haven't had much of an opportunity so far on tour and I was happy to let him have a turn.

Down at the ground I was told there had been a phone call for me from Declan's father. Apparently there had been 'a serious problem'. I felt sick just thinking about the possibilities and hoping against hope that the little battler would pull through. When I finally got through on the phone it turned out they just weren't happy with their tickets, having expected seats in the under-cover section.

England won the toss and batted first with Tugga setting an aggressive field of 4 slips and a gully. It paid off with Trescothick going for a duck in Pigeon's first over. From there the wheels pretty much fell off for England as they slumped to be all out for 176 in the 43rd over. Our boys had little trouble knocking off the target, with Gilly and Punter both notching up half centuries. Symo played well although, as I commented to Tugga, I felt his feet were a little slow and he struggled to really adapt to the slower wickets, often chopping down on the ball at the last moment in a manner that could only be described as 'technically flawed' and typical of a batsman not really comfortable at this level of the game. Still, 103 not out is a pretty decent score and hopefully the young player gained something valuable from the experience.

Victory came in just the 30th over and naturally we were keen to enjoy the occasion with a few thirst-quenchers in the rooms after play. However, the celebrations were modest by our normal standards and most of the guys were back at our hotel within the regulation 72 hours.

Friday June 22

With the one-day final set for tomorrow there was a real intensity to training this morning with everyone keen to catch the eye of the selectors. As far as us batsmen go, Marto's solid form so far makes him an almost certainty for a berth, while Symo was again looking impressive in the nets. But of course my long record of experience and dedication couldn't be easily overlooked. Obviously it was a tough call who to leave out and you could see Tugga and Gilly deep in conversation, but it was a little hard to make out what they were saying, even with the binoculars. Eventually at lunch the decision came through — I was in the team! As far as our bowlers went, it was Flem who missed out. The big Victorian took it well — I think. It was hard to tell as no one saw him for the next three days.

Back at the hotel I received another call from Declan's father, this time wanting reserved seating to the final. When I explained tickets had all been sold out he got quite aggressive, telling me the disappointment could well trigger a cardiac episode and kill the young lad. I promised to see what I could do.

The team meeting tonight was enhanced by a video presentation featuring some inspirational footage of our recent victories intertwined with scenes from an American movie about call-girls who stow away on a navy submarine. It certainly had the boys fired up and ready to go. After everyone calmed down Tugga reminded us that it was the little things, the one-percenters that would really make a victory possible. He concluded by saying he wanted us all totally committed and focused when we walked out onto the Oval tomorrow. At which point Gilly reminded him the game was actually at Lords. Tugga didn't look happy.

Saturday June 23

Australia vs Pakistan
One-Day International Final, Lords

Strict security measures were in place for the final here at Lords with matches, flags, banners, musical instruments and 'anything else that might be a missile' banned. Yet for some reason firecrackers didn't seem to fit this description and there were explosions going off from the moment we arrived at the ground. The Pakis won the toss and surprisingly decided to bat first, as they did here in the World Cup final a few years back. The decision was equally unsuccessful this time round with the local favourites all out for just 152 runs in the 42nd over. The star for us was Warney who took three important wickets including that of Inzamam-ul-Haq who, after being adjudged lbw for just 23, refused to budge, glaring back down the pitch at our Sheik of Tweak. No doubt he was just a little confused as to the direction of the change rooms and naturally we were happy to show him the way.

Dignity, restraint and good sportsmanship were all hallmarks of our win.

Chasing a small total is never easy and when Junior went for 36 I found myself strolling to the pitch determined not to let this opportunity slip. As a ground Lords is not quite what you'd expect, and there's a distinct slope of more than two metres running from the square leg boundary on your left to the other side. I remember the first time I walked out here as part of the Australian youth squad thinking, 'No more pre-match drinking.' But neither the slope nor the fanatical Paki fans could bother me today as Gilly and I set about knocking off the required runs, a feat achieved in just the 26th over. As we scampered through for the winning run I couldn't help but give a little 'victory' jab with my bat and the fact it connected with Wasim Akram's ribcage was purely accidental.

And there it was — another one-day series victory for Australia. Looking back, it all happened so quickly. One moment we were walking out onto the field, the next I was on the balcony holding the man of the match award. (It had actually been given to Gilly but by this stage he was too pissed to realise.) The only sour note for the day occurred during the presentation ceremony when some lunatic threw a can of VB at Bevo. I remember thinking it had to have been a Paki fan. What Australian would throw a full can of beer away? Naturally Tugga was furious, as were Foster's who felt the coverage given to this piece of rival product placement quite unacceptable. Tugga immediately led us off the field and into the rooms where Bevo was treated by a doctor and the presentation ceremony completed. Then it was time to sit back and truly enjoy the special feeling that comes with a hard-fought win. Punter led us in a rousing chorus of 'Under the Southern Cross' that was belted out with great passion and little tune by us all. Looking round it was incredible to see the various expressions on the guy's faces, ranging from sheer jubilation from some of the younger blokes, to pure relief and contentment from Tugga and Gilly. It was a little difficult to make out Warney's expression as by this time he was lying face down under the physio's bench.

During the speeches that followed Tugga spoke highly of our 'dirt-trackers', the guys who rarely get a game on tour but who are forever willing to put in for the team, maintain a positive outlook and encourage us all. As a special thankyou, a few of them were even allowed into the rooms for this part of the speech.

Sunday June 24

Not surprisingly the celebrations went well into the night as we toasted our one-day final win in the rooms and then later back at the hotel. There were quite a few emotional fans waiting for us in the bar along with a few ex-players, including my old mate Merv, who was so choked up he actually had tears in his eyes. I found out later that he'd had two grand on us to lose the match.

Several newspapers this morning published security camera photos of yesterday's mystery beer-can thrower. The images are pretty grainy but I'm fairly certain I recognise the face — it's Declan's dad. I've notified the authorities and also done a little investigating of my own. Turns out his 'life-threatening' heart condition isn't so serious after all and he's actually in no real danger of dying. Unless I happen to bump into him. The other good news to come out of yesterday was that Inzamam-ul-Haq has been fined half his match fee and suspended for 2 one-day internationals for dissent, loitering after being given out lbw. Now every cricketer has at one point in their career hung around for a few seconds after being given a dodgy decision, but this bloke was still out there glaring down the pitch when we were completing our victory lap.

It's always a relief when the team bus arrives at our hotel.

Today we make the trip down south for our next tour match but sadly not everyone will be going. Medical reports on Nathan Bracken's shoulder injury have confirmed that he has little chance of playing again on tour. To see the hurt and disappointment on the face of any cricketer in this situation is really gut wrenching, especially a bloke like Bracko who has slotted into the squad so well. However, it was felt by everyone concerned that it would be better if he left immediately rather than face the slow torture of just hanging around on the fringes, so the bus pulled over and we dropped him at a Caltex service station before heading off down the road. His place will be taken by Queensland paceman Ashley Noffke.

We were also joined today by a few Test arrivals in the form of Lang, Slats, Funky and Katto. It can be tough for these late arrivals as by now all the good seats on the team bus have been taken and the new boys are forced to sit down the back or next to Buck. Speaking of our coach, he was looking very pleased with himself tonight, having called a team meeting at which a comprehensive training and fitness schedule was outlined. The fact Buck was the only one who showed up to the meeting didn't seem to bother him at all.

After a few weeks on tour, we all decide our favourite position on the team bus.

Monday June 25

Australia vs MCC XI
Arundel Castle Ground, Day 1

Even though the three-day tour match beginning here at the castle ground is traditionally a relaxed affair there is still a lot riding on it, especially with the arrival of our Test-only players like Slats and Lang who are keen to cement their place in the team. Following the success of guys like Marto, and of course *myself*, in the one-day series there's a bit of pressure on us all, and with only two lead-up matches before the first Test everyone will be keen for the chance to push their case. A situation like this could easily lead to tension within a squad but fortunately we're all good mates and our main concern is of course that the team does well. At least, that's what we tell each other.

It was officially the hottest day of the year over here — a scorching 29 degrees — as we won the toss and elected to bat. Unfortunately the home team had a Queensland bowler by the name of Joe Dawes in their line-up and this bloke played havoc with our top order. Slats, Lang and Marto all went for single figures and by the time I strolled to the crease things were looking a little dire for us Aussies. I managed to see off the first few overs and get a feel for the pitch, watching every ball onto my bat and punishing the loose deliveries as I moved steadily into

I was out a few balls later after nodding off at the crease.

the thirties. After weeks of sub-arctic weather it was tough concentrating in the warm conditions and I had to work hard not to let my focus slip. Of course that's what cricket is all about, the ability to concentrate and focus for long periods, whether you're building a big innings, fielding in slips or just listening to one of Tugga's pre-match addresses.

Speaking of our skipper, he was at the other end on 45 when we went to lunch, an excellent spread featuring smoked salmon, quiche, locally baked pies, custard and cheesecake. Unfortunately we both overindulged, with Tugga out first ball after lunch and me following a few overs later after nodding off momentarily at the crease. A big 168 not out from Test-hopeful Katto and a 69 from Warney took our final score to a quite respectable 390. The MCC XI reached 6 for 82 in reply with Funky, Flem, Dizzy and Warney all sharing in the wickets. One interesting moment took place late in the day when opener Richardson edged a ball from Flem through to our reserve keeper, Wade Seccombe, who dived full length and appeared to just get a glove on it. But instead of joining the rest of us in appealing Secco went straight over to the umpire and said, 'I'm not sure if it carried.' As a sportsman it was a wonderful thing to do. As an Australian it was an absolute disgrace and I doubt he'll play for this country again.

After play both teams had their photo taken with the Earl of Arundel who introduced himself as 'Eddie'. Such informality was refreshing to see and it was a pity the gesture was not reciprocated by Tugga, who insisted on being addressed as 'Captain Waugh'.

Tuesday June 26

Australia vs MCC XI
Arundel Castle Ground, Day 2

Before play this morning the Australian team was given a personal tour of Arundel Castle by the Earl himself who showed us its fascinating collection of artefacts and antiques, all in superb condition, beautifully presented and, we quickly discovered, nailed to the wall. A crossbow used by one of the Earl's ancestors caught the attention of Pigeon who, keen student of history that he is, inquired of our host, 'Reckon you could drop a feral pig with this sucker?'

When play commenced the MCC XI managed to add just 42 more runs, ending their innings on 124. Enforcing a follow-on was not an option as Tugga elected for some more batting practice. Unfortunately Slats failed again (17), as did Lang who made a first-ball duck. With our second innings looking shaky it was time for someone to put up their hand and that person was me — caught behind off the glove fending at a short one. Fortunately Tugga came out firing, knocking up 105 runs in quick time to record his 64th first-class century. He was ably supported by Marto and we ended the day on 8 for 294.

There is a bit of tension amongst our top order with Slats (7 and 17), Lang (4 and 0) and myself (31 and 2) conscious of blokes like Marto and Katto knocking on the door, but of course the main aim is retaining the Ashes, not individual glory,

We enjoyed our brief tour of historic Arundel Castle.

No-one likes to see a fellow player hurt — unless, of course, he's a member of the England team.

and we just want to see the best team selected. Provided it contains us.

Tonight saw the lads in formal gear as we headed off for the traditional MCC welcoming dinner. This is a very stiff-upper-lip, tedious affair with us players again split up, one per table and forced to endure an entire evening of hearing pipe-smoking Pommy geriatrics make quips like, 'Good luck — but not too much!', or 'Take it easy on our boys', or the favourite, 'You've brought the weather with you haven't you?' At one point I found myself stuck between two old codgers who trotted out the usual 'ugly Australian' cliches, in particular that we drink and sledge a lot. I tried to respond in a calm and rational manner, which wasn't easy as I was pretty pissed by this stage, but couldn't seem to shake their opinions. Personally, I think this 'sledging' stereotype goes back to the Chappell era, but to be honest it no longer applies. Sledging is simply not a major part of our current playing policy and anyone who says differently can get f*#ked.

Wednesday June 27

Australia vs MCC XI
Arundel Castle Ground, Day 3

It was a bunch of bleary-eyed, rather hung-over Aussie cricketers who made their way to the castle ground this morning for the final day's play. We decided to retire on our overnight score — no one could actually remember what it was but it seemed like a reasonable idea. The home side opened their second innings and Funky got rid of Mutjaba for 22 which brought a bloke by the name of David Ward to the crease. This guy was 40 years old and had the physique of Merv Hughes during an extended off-season break. But to put it bluntly, the fat bastard belted the daylights out of us. Funky was forced to switch from medium-pace to off-spin and then to fine leg where he was out of harm's way. Even Warney got belted for 18 off one over before eventually knocking the bloke over for 57.

Shortly after lunch (full details of which can be found in the supplement on p. 233), Lang copped a nasty blow to his wrist from Jimmy Adams while fielding at short leg and left the field looking shaken. He immediately had ice treatment applied but now only has one day to recover before our next tour match. Naturally we top-order batsmen were all very concerned for his health and told him to take as much time off as he wanted and that there would be no shame in sitting out the match or the first Test, or flying home, or even retiring, but the big West Australian seemed determined to fight his way back.

The MCC XI were eventually dismissed for 280, giving us a morale-boosting victory and the opportunity to enjoy a few well-earned drinks after play. But with another big match just a few days off Tugga insisted we keep the celebrations low key and to this end he demanded each member of the squad hand in their passport.

It was great catching up with Ros's sister Maureen who now lives here in England.

Thursday June 28

We travelled down here to Chelmsford last night and enjoyed a good evening out at a local Italian restaurant before heading back to the hotel bar for a couple of cleansing ales. As usual there were a lot of fans hanging around wanting a chat or a photograph, which can be a bit of a pain when you're trying to relax. One young kid, an Aussie, kept trying to join the boys and wouldn't take a subtle hint so I was forced to tell him 'to piss off' in no uncertain terms. Turned out this morning his name is Ashley Noffke, our new replacement for Bracko. I may have to apologise although frankly he should have been wearing a name tag. Speaking of apologies, there was an article in this morning's *Telegraph* about Lang's injury and his chances of playing tomorrow. Gilly is quoted as saying 'I reckon you could saw his arm off and he'd still play!' to which I allegedly added 'and just as badly!' It was *obviously* meant as a *joke*, as I've tried explaining to Lang all morning, but he's not leaving his room which is kind of awkward because he's locked me in here with him.

Tugga is in such good form that he has decided to hand over the reins to Gilly for tomorrow's match while he and the family enjoy a visit to EuroDisney in France. Of course, had we not been playing so well Tugga naturally would have stayed and Gilly would have taken Lynette and the kids to Paris. Warney is also taking the match off, leaving senior control of the team pretty much to me and Gilly. Our first step was to cancel training and organise a trip in to London to watch the tennis.

With several wins under our belt we all realised a long meeting was not required tonight. Unfortunately no one told Buck who insisted on another gruelling 90-minute stats session.

Friday June 29

Australia vs Essex
County Ground, Day 1

The one thing you're guaranteed to find during any Ashes series is a crowd full of colourful characters and one such gentlemen is without doubt Reginald Tuckfield. Reginald, or 'Reg' as he is known, is a local legend here at the county ground, having occupied the same seat and worn the same brown jacket at every match for the past 23 years. It's a delightful tale but one with a slightly sad ending, as ground authorities recently discovered the bloke has been dead for the past seven years.

We won the toss and elected to use the opportunity for some much-needed batting practice. Unfortunately Slats and Hados were quickly back in the pavilion, courtesy of a fiery opening spell from Ilott and Bishop. With pressure mounting for Test selection the last thing Lang wanted this morning was to get out first ball, which is good because he got out second ball, registering yet another duck against his name. Punter and I managed to steady the ship and by lunch we were comfortably placed on 3 for 136.

At the team meeting last night we had discussed the fact that England captain Nasser Hussain would be making his come-back today after missing several weeks with a broken thumb. The plan was to target him early, not let him have any time in the middle and if possible inflict a few psychological scars. It was even suggested that a little blow on the fingers might help! I admit now in hindsight that deliberately dropping a salad bowl on his hand during the luncheon interval was perhaps taking this plan a little too far, but the opportunity just seemed too good to miss.

I went for 62 shortly after lunch, trying to push the run rate along, leaving the door open for Marto (114*) and Gilly (150*) to really take the Essex attack apart. We eventually declared on 405, giving us a few overs at the home side late in the day, a tactic that paid off when Pigeon had their opener, Grayson, caught behind for 0.

Lang celebrates surviving his first ball.

There's no doubting how much our wives and girlfriends enjoy being part of an Ashes tour.

Hussain managed to survive his short stint at the crease, getting off the mark with a thumping 6 off Pigeon. I tell you what, there's nothing quite like the face of our fiery paceman when he's hit out of the park. He'll glare at the batsman, mouth a few pleasantries, kick the ground and spit, often simultaneously, in a display of pure aggro that says 'I'm gonna knock you're f*#king head off.' Of course it's pure theatre, designed to intimidate the batsman and deep down we all know Pigeon's an old softie. He's often the first to run in after decking a bloke with a bouncer and check if he's still breathing. That said, Hussain didn't attempt any more boundaries and they went to stumps on 1 for 16.

Back at the hotel I decided to phone Ros and the kids back in Australia. They were spending the week at her parents' house, which was good because it gave me the opportunity to reverse the charges.

Quite a few of the boys have their partners over here and it's great to see the girls enjoying part of the tour. This wasn't always the case and not so many years back players' partners were not even allowed to visit during an Ashes campaign. My wife Ros was one of the first to challenge this attitude and back in the early '90s she went so far as to organise a wives and girlfriends' support group. Unfortunately it ran into trouble at the very first meeting when a certain middle-order batsman's wife *and* girlfriend both showed up. As you could imagine, not only did this sort of thing create a lot of tension, it played havoc with the catering arrangements.

Saturday June 30

Australia vs Essex
County Ground, Day 2

It turns out we're not the only Aussie cricketers over here at the moment, with our women's team currently doing battle as well. In the paper this morning the captain of England's team, Clare Connor, has come out quite strongly accusing the Aussie girls of being very bad sledgers. According to Connor (I don't know if she has a nickname), the Aussie slips fielders have been saying stuff like 'Jeez, check out the arse on her', and 'Hey, do you have to be ugly to get into this side?' It's certainly given me a new-found respect for our Aussie girls and who knows, I might just try out a few of these 'pleasantries' myself.

An inspired spell of fast bowling from Dizzy this morning had the Essex boys on the back foot, with the big South Australian taking 5 wickets for the innings. He

It's not often you'll see an Australian batsman in tears, but when Hados went for 98 it was hard to hold back.

was well backed up by Funky, who took 3, and Pigeon who claimed the vital scalp of Hussain, although I must claim some credit for this wicket. The England captain was looking set for a big knock when, just as Pigeon was coming in, I commented from short leg, 'Check out the arse on her.' He looked up and was clean bowled.

Perhaps our only worry on the bowling front is Binger, who continues to be expensive, his 7 overs going for 41 runs. We eventually bundled the home side out for 231, leaving ourselves a few good hours for batting practice. Slats knocked up a quick-fire 58 and Hados fell just two short of a century, holing out to off-spinner Peter Such for 98. Having been there I can tell you there's nothing more frustrating for a batsman than losing your wicket in the nineties, and we could tell Hados was a little pissed off with himself from the moment his bat came flying through the visitors' dressing-room window.

Bing was sent in after Gilly decided to move our bowlers up the order to give them some batting practice. It was also felt that as he'd conceded so many runs he should bloody well get out there and make some. He ended on 7* along with Lang on 10*, who is desperate for a big knock tomorrow.

This evening Punter took a bunch of us to the Romford greyhounds where we enjoyed a few drinks and a few laughs as we watched our 'favourites' lose race after race. Luckily Hados picked a winner in the last event, otherwise we would have had a lot of explaining to do when the other boys asked what happened to the social committee funds. After a big day in the field I was pleased to report I felt no stiffness or pain during the evening. Mind you, by this stage I was pretty pissed.

Sunday July 1

Australia vs Essex, County Ground, Day 3

I woke this morning with a stuffy nose and sore throat, the start I fear of a cold, that had me searching through my toilet bag for something that might ease the symptoms. A large dose of Vitamin C and a switch to Benson & Hedges extra milds for the next few days will hopefully do the trick.

Settling into the rooms I could tell that Lang was looking worried, so as the big fella padded up I went over and had a few words, reminding him that success was all about confidence and not letting negative thoughts enter your head. Just to reinforce this message, I called out to him as he walked onto the field, 'Don't listen to what people say about you not being able to play spin!' To be honest, the big fella struggled, taking 98 minutes to add another 7 runs before falling to former Test off-spinner Peter Such.

I cop a nasty blow . . .

Warney does a quick count of the damage.

The rest of the day was not all that exciting as Gilly insisted we bat on to give everyone a bit of time in the middle. My cold was feeling worse so I moved down the order while Dizzy, Punter, Funky and Marto took us to 9 (declared) for 569. The crowd here at Chelmsford weren't all that impressed. I guess they expected a sporting declaration from us around lunchtime and several spectators were slow-hand clapping, fairly vocal about our tactics and becoming abusive. This is a side of cricket I find quite disappointing, the general decline in crowd behaviour. Back in Australia my daughters often like to come and see me play and sometimes I shudder to think of them sitting in the outer with all that offensive language flying about. Fortunately much of it comes from them, which softens the impact a little.

After a few energy-replenishing fluids another bus trip saw us checking into the

Birmingham Hyatt, a slightly more up-market form of accommodation than our previous hotel. This place has a palatial lobby, so huge you could kick a footy in here — in fact, several of the boys did and managed to bring down a chandelier, putting an end to that particular activity.

By this stage of the tour a lot of the guys' families have joined us and there were some pretty happy reunions taking place at the hotel, especially for those blokes with young kids. Of course it's not all smooth sailing having children around on tour and you've got to be careful of situations, such as when a crying baby might keep a batsman up the night before an important game. But generally these sorts of problems can be easily prevented with simple solutions like the wife and baby sleeping in the car during Test fixtures.

When you think back to the old days, it's incredible to realise how an Ashes squad would often be away from home for five months with no personal contact between husband and wife apart from the odd letter. They didn't even have Hero-grams back then. Dads would get back and actually have to be introduced to their kids. Fathers are now so much more actively involved in child-raising, but this is a fairly recent phenomenon. I remember when Ros had our first daughter, I raised quite a few eyebrows by actually taking paternity leave. It was something almost unheard of back then, but for me the decision was simple. I took the day off work, no questions asked, dropped a bunch of plastic balloons at the hospital's reception desk and then celebrated with a round of golf.

Monday July 2

With just three days to go until the first Test we woke to the bombshell that Lang has been dropped, his place to be taken by Western Australian team-mate Damien Martyn. As you could imagine it's always difficult telling a good mate and dedicated team man that he has lost his place in the side, and I'm sure Buck felt pretty upset as he slid the note under his door last night. Not half as upset as Junior of course, who accidentally received the note. The mistake was eventually cleared up and Lang given the news. Not that he wouldn't have seen it coming. His string of low scores, poor footwork and the way we've all been falling silent whenever he entered the room must have been a give-away that something was in the wind. The simple fact is Lang has been in the country just nine days, but in that time he has failed four times (five if you count the ten-pin bowling night he organised on behalf of the team social committee). Of course, Lang's a hard worker and a great team man and we know he'll contribute to this Ashes campaign. It's very important in times like this for a player not to feel he is useless to the squad and we all made a point of dropping off some laundry outside his door this morning just to keep him involved.

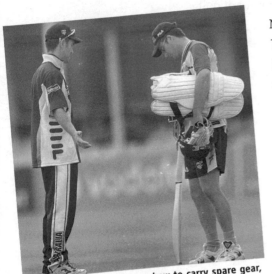

Tugga demonstrates to Lang how to carry spare gear, just one of the duties he'll now be responsible for as 12th man

With Lang out Punter moves to the Number 3 spot and Marto takes over at Six. There have also been some changes in the England squad with Mark Ramprakash ruled out of the first Test team with a hamstring injury. He was of course recalled to cover for the injured Graham Thorpe. Luckily our injury woes are a lot less severe: I've still got a slight cold and Funky's latest hair-colouring job has been a disaster, but neither should keep us from playing.

On a long tour it's important to keep fitness and training sessions fun if players are to enjoy going along. One way to achieve this is to cancel them.

Tuesday July 3

Our final workout before the Ashes series begins took place in sultry conditions. We started by warming up on the outfield, then the batsmen moved to the nets to face an hour of bowling from our boys as well as some local net bowlers. There was an interesting bunch here today: Joe Dawes (last seen at Arundel two weeks ago) and Hados's brother Gary, as well as this fat, glasses-wearing Paki who got really excited if one of his wrong 'uns so much as landed on the wicket. I was happy with my practice form, concentrating on footwork and balance that, to a cricketer, are critical qualities whether at the crease or just on the way home from a big night out.

Lang waited until we had all finished before starting his net session. The poor bloke's still shellshocked and obviously not that keen to speak with anyone right now, although I do believe Tugga, Buck and Gilly had a chat with the big Western Australian this morning. Tugga did the talking, Gilly and Buck held him down. It's an exciting time for Marto who, as Tugga summed up so well over lunch, is playing this Test not because someone is injured but because Lang is in such shit form.

Unwinding in the hotel pool.

141

Marto is a super-fit professional who trains hard, has a controlled diet and keeps a low profile. Yet somehow he still manages to fit into the Aussie squad. It's been quite a transformation for the talented Western Australian, who actually toured here in '93 as part of the Ashes squad. Back then his general behaviour was so poor he was actually grounded and confined to the team hotel after hours. (So too were six other members of the touring squad, which meant that the best parties tended to take place back there.) His nicknames used to be Party Animal and Wild Child but he's now had them officially changed to Marto.

England today called up three players to bolster its depleted line-up. Mark Butcher, Robert Croft and newcomer Usman Afzaal will come in to replace Thorpe (torn calf muscle), Ramprakash (hamstring strain) and Michael Vaughan (rostered day off).

Our traditional pre-Test team dinner was held tonight at a local Italian restaurant personally recommended by Warney and I think we all enjoyed our visit to Pizza Hut, tucking into some cheese pizzas and large plates of lasagne. There's a great feeling amongst the squad, a determination to do well. The evening was further enhanced when Buck played us a motivational tape he'd put together featuring some of our recent Ashes triumphs that certainly got everyone fired up. The mood was slightly brought down when he then offered copies for sale at $27.95 each, but the boys still bought up big.

Wednesday July 4

We took the day off from training but did go down to the ground at Edgbaston for the presentation of the International Cricket Council Test World Championship Trophy. It's a pretty impressive looking mace in silver and gold, bearing the logos of all Test-playing countries (although South Africa's logo appeared to be attached only temporarily) and Australia is the first country to receive the award. As a symbol, it was a stark reminder to the Poms

A proud moment as we hold the ICC Test World Championship Trophy.

of our superiority. They were training nearby and even though they didn't attend the presentation ceremony, we did a victory lap of the nets just to make the point clear.

My pre-match routine is pretty settled after all these years: a haircut, massage and a visit to Ladbrokes. Here I discovered they are offering 15–1 on Australia winning the series 5–0, attractive odds for sure but, as they say at table-top dancing clubs, 'You can look but you better not touch!'*

A quiet meal tonight was preceded by a team meeting and you could tell the Test series was about to begin as we all met in the one room, a change from the phone conferencing system we'd been experimenting with during the county fixtures.

Back in my room I received a phone call from Ros, who sounded a little down. Apparently we were burgled last night and the scumbags took our DVD player, TV, stereo and quite a bit of jewellery. Thank goodness they didn't get into my trophy room (it's fully alarmed), and my memorabilia collection remains intact. On top of the burglary, Ros's brother has had a stroke and is in hospital, the car's broken down and both kids have been suspended from school again for smoking. I told Ros I had a cold and was a little worried about my footwork, but she didn't seem that interested. I really felt she could have been more supportive.

* Not that I've been to many such establishments in recent times. Some of the younger single blokes like the occasional night out there, but the last time I went along was during a stop-over in Hong Kong. I must say, those Chinese dancers are very skilful, not only managing all the exotic moves but performing them while balancing on top of a lazy susan.

Thursday July 5

Australia vs England
1st Test, Edgbaston, Day 1

This is it boys, the start of the Ashes,
We're not playing for prizes or even cash(es),
We're here for Australia, a land that we know,
As into battle, eleven warriors go.
Let's not forget Lang, left out of the side,
He'll carry our drinks with customary pride . . .

(Jason Gillespie, read before play, Day 1)

Well, this is it, the start of the Ashes series, the pinnacle of any cricketing career. Which makes it all the more surprising that so many of us slept in and almost missed the team bus.

Down at the ground we began the task of settling into the rooms, hanging up gear in the overhead lockers, whitening boots and making a few last-minute sponsorship deals. With a 10.05 am start, our warm-ups commenced at 9.15 and involved a few light stretches before heading back inside and switching the urn on. Players all have different ways of relaxing before a big match. Blokes like Dizzy listen to heavy metal music through their personal stereos. Hados likes to walk around nude rehearsing various shots (you don't want to be there for the sweep). Meanwhile Pigeon loves nothing more than a good book. Unfortunately there was no one free to read him one this morning.

Tugga won the toss, an event marred slightly by rival captain Nasser Hussain walking out onto the pitch wearing a Vodaphone cap instead of the more traditional baggy blue. Quite a few conservative commentators were outraged by this break with tradition but my sympathies lie with Hussain. Sponsors have to be looked after, a point I remember making years ago to Ros just before our wedding when she insisted I remove the Victoria Bitter T-shirt. As I explained to her then, 'Sweetheart, this T-shirt's paying for half the bloody reception, now shut up and get into the church.'

With the decision made to bowl first our quicks limbered up as they visualised the task ahead of them. The rest of us sat back and visualised lunch. Then it was time to start play.

The England captain copped a lot of flak for walking out to toss in a sponsor's cap . . .

But if you ask me, you've got to look after your sponsors.

" Dizzy struck early, taking the wicket of Trescothick with the first ball of his second over. We had a few more chances after this, but unfortunately Butcher and Atherton were both dropped by the same player — there's no need to name names, our keeper knows who he is. Atherton was also lucky to survive a confident lbw shout from Pigeon in his 3rd over. It was so confident it went for several minutes and nearly blew up a pitch microphone. But the Poms held out to be 1 for 106 just one over before lunch. It was then Tugga tossed Warney the ball and our legendary leggie obliged by taking the wicket of Butcher with just his second delivery. //

During the next session the Poms pretty much collapsed to be 7 for 191 by tea. Pigeon joined the carnage, knocking over their captain Hussain with a morale-destroying burst of pace and despite a last-minute fight-back by Caddick (49*), we had them all out for just 294.

Our first innings got off to a flying start courtesy of Slats who smashed 18 off the first over from Gough. Punter was unlucky to be given out lbw to Gough on 11, especially as later the TV replays apparently showed it was a no-ball. I say 'apparently' as by the time they were being shown, Punter had ripped the dressing-room TV from its bracket and tossed it into one of the shower cubicles. At the end of the day we were well placed on 2 for 133.

If one thing could sum up the difference between the two teams today, it was late this afternoon when Test debutant Usman Afzaal dropped a sharp catch at square leg off Slats. Both the crowd and his team-mates gave him hearty applause

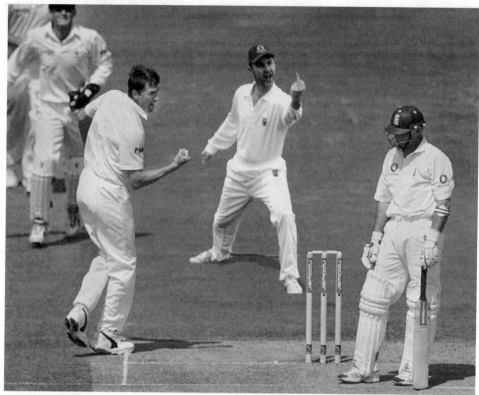

From the start we could tell this series would be played in the right spirit.

for his efforts. Now, if we Aussies drop a catch, no matter how difficult, we certainly don't expect applause. We'd be lucky to get a stony silence broken only by a couple of quite personal comments.

Back at the hotel there was quite a contingent of ex-Aussie players keen to have a chat and share a few beers. AB, Tubby, Heals and Boonie are all over here leading tour groups, while Greg Chappell and Henry Lawson are doing some commentary work. It was good catching up with these legends of the game, many of whom are good mates. About the only one I never really got on with was Henry, and that was for obvious reasons. Before I even met him I'd heard the rumours about his 'preferences' and sure enough they turned out to be true. Now I'm a typical Aussie bloke and I simply don't have time for his type, especially on a long overseas tour. Sure, you can give me all that politically correct crap about 'freedom of choice' and 'lifestyle decisions' but I'm sorry — there is no place in Australian cricket for a teetotaller.

Friday July 6

Australia vs England
1st Test, Edgbaston, Day 2

Well the Poms are on the back foot so let's keep 'em all that way,
Let's really put the boot in and for their mistakes make 'em pay,
Grind 'em into the wicket 'til they're bleeding from the ears,
Rip their guts out, slit their throats and stick . . .

(Brett Lee, read before being taken away and sedated, Day 2)

When we pulled up in the bus this morning we were greeted by eerie, foggy conditions, not helped by the fact Slats and Warney were both smoking like Indian schoolboys. With two wickets down and still 160 runs behind, it was important we got off to a good start, but it wasn't long before we heard the familiar mid-wicket cry from Slats of 'Yes! No! No! Yes! Yes! Yes! No!!, suggesting our star opener still hadn't quite sorted out his running between wickets. Unfortunately Slats was bowled by Gough off just the 4th ball of the day, catching us all a little by surprise.

I was in the dunny having a nervous one, Tugga was still sorting out his CD collection and Punter was up on a chair trying to tune in Sky Channel on the new TV when the wicket fell. Junior was the next to go, caught behind after he momentarily lost sight of the ball behind Caddick's ear. Tugga and I then steadied the ship, not an easy task given the poor light and barrage of short-pitched bowling we copped. We both took a few nasty blows to the body but the Poms couldn't tie us down, Tugga notching up an unbeaten century before bad light and rain finally forced everyone off the field in search of a cold one. Which unfortunately turned out to be the showers.

During a Test we like to increase team unity by making sure the players socialise together and a few of the boys were keen to go out for a drink tonight, but others wanted to stay in and

We were a little surprised when Slats was bowled off the fourth ball of the day. But not as surprised as him.

One of the finest batsmen this country has ever produced. And in the foreground, Steve Waugh.

have a quiet night at the hotel bar. It's times like this when I think how tough Tugga's job really is. As captain he has to constantly bring together twelve different personalities. Or twenty if Slats is playing. In the end it was decided to stay in which suited me as I was feeling a little sore after facing the Pommy pace brigade today. Of course Tugga often says that if you've got a few bruises it's a good thing — it means you've spent a bit of time in the middle. It's much the same attitude Punter applies to a night out in Kings Cross.

Saturday July 7

Australia vs England
1st Test, Edgbaston, Birmingham, Day 3

A is for 'awesome', the way we like to play,
Hard and fast and furious right throughout the day.
B is for our 'batting' strength, the key to making runs,
Whether sixes, fours or singles, we all like getting tons.
C is for 'cricket', it's the game we . . .

(Simon Katich, read before being told there would now be a time limit on all poems, Day 3)

The first two hours of this morning's session were rained out, leaving us players with little more to do than sit around the rooms playing 500. In between card games we had the 'pleasure' of signing a mountain of bats for various sponsors and charities, a task universally hated by all players, so much so that on most tours we tend to get our room attendants and net bowlers to do the signing for us. But the rain delay this morning gave us no excuses and so it was on with the job while outside the crowd were entertained by a replay on the scoreboard screen of England defeating Australia in the so-called 'unloseable' Headingley Test of 1981. Honestly, the Poms trot this tape out so often I'm surprised it hasn't worn out by now. It's like cricket pornography for them and whenever there's a national crisis — foot and mouth, floods, Prince Phillip making a public statement — they screen Botham's famous rampage. It may have fired up the crowd but it only served to harden our resolve to get out there and thrash their pale Pommy arses, an opportunity we eventually had when the rain eased off around 11.30.

Tugga and I resumed our places in the middle of the pitch with Australia just 38 runs ahead. A few balls later Tugga resumed his place in the dressing-room, lbw to Gough after adding just 4 runs to his overnight score. It was then up to Gilly and me to prevent a collapse and give us a decent first-innings lead. It wasn't easy batting, given the low light and the fierce bowling from Gough and more specifically, Caddick, who had copped a fair bit of short-stuff during his big innings on the first day and was obviously keen to settle the ledger. There was little sympathy from the England players in close and even when I copped a nasty blow to the elbow no one seemed that concerned. All I heard was 'Get on with it ya' weak shit', which was a

The three century-makers from Edgbaston. Gilly, Tugga and you can just make out my arse in the background — they didn't tell me we were having a photo shoot.

pretty hurtful comment, especially as it came from Gilly. Speaking of my batting partner, he too was playing well, racing towards a ton in typical flamboyant style. I played the anchor role to his show-off innings. I mean, it's easy to look good when you hog the strike and smash a few boundaries, but the real class is shown by the bloke who works the singles, shares the strike and plays responsibly. Which is exactly what I did, racing to my first Test century of the tour shortly after tea. I fell a few runs later, according to some commentators after 'relaxing too much'. Okay, the one-handed sweep shot may not be all that common, but on 105 who gives a rats arse? Gilly meanwhile blazed his way to 152, ensuring our massive final total of 576.

With one session remaining the Poms came out to bat and Tugga immediately set a very attacking field. No fine leg, just a bat-pad patrolling the on side, seven blokes on the off and one back in the rooms helping to set up chairs for the team singalong. Things went according to plan with Pigeon's bunny Atherton falling to him for just 4. Trescothick and Butcher were both looking pretty shaky when poor light eventually ended play. If it hadn't, then poor batting surely would have.

With the very real feeling that a Test win could be just a day or so away we decided to stop back and enjoy a few 'quiet ones' in the rooms after play. Beer flowed freely and there will no doubt be a few bleary eyes tomorrow. Just better make sure I don't sleep in and miss the bus.

The F*#king A*sey C*#t Clock
Collector's Timepiece

January 18, 2001. Bowler Shane Warne is hit over the boundary by young Zimbabwean batsman Stuart Carlisle. Standing over the stump microphone he is clearly heard uttering the immortal curse 'You f*#king a*sey c*#t!'

Now this special moment in cricket history is preserved for all time with the officially authorised F*#king A*sey C*#nt Clock. Hear Warney let fly every hour, on the hour, with this beautifully crafted timepiece.

(Above) A moment of triumph after the '99 World Cup soon turned to tragedy when Warney shook the bottle a little too vigorously . . .

(Right) It's why I always stick to beer.

A moment of victory for us all.

As a member of the Australian team you're always learning. Today's lesson — never put a team shirt in the wash with blue training shorts.

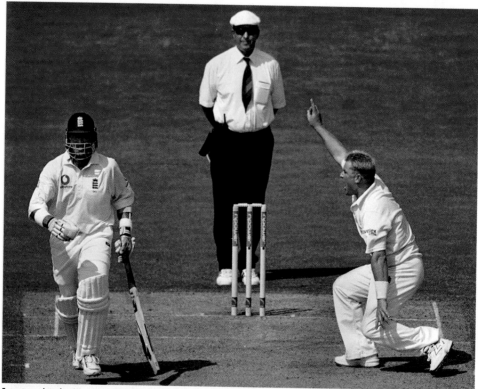

In a novel twist Warney will often bypass the umpire and appeal directly to the television commentary box.

Gilly, Warney, Punter and I enjoy the fresh air of London's Hyde Park. (That's me on the bench.)

Sunday July 8

Australia vs England
1st Test, Edgbaston, Day 4

The Poms thought they were good and could beat anybody,
But they didn't count on Tugga or Gilly or Toddy.
It's time to let them know that the Aussies have landed,
And then we can sing 'Under the Southern Cross' we standed . . .

(Ricky Ponting, read before play, Day 4)

No chance of W Todd missing the team bus this morning as I somehow managed to fall asleep on it last night. When we pulled into the Edgbaston carpark at 9.05 am there was a small crowd of about thirty fans braving the cold in the hope of that all-important signature from a favourite player. Constantly signing autographs can be a bit of a pain but the way I see it, if someone's keen enough to sit around for hours waiting for a signature who are we to say 'No'? We get our driver to do that.

Perhaps my strongest memory of the day was the sight of Punter up on the physio's bench, a beloved Cascade in one hand, belting out the team song with patriotic pride. It's a scene I've been privileged to witness on many occasions, only this time was quite unique as it was only 10.30 am and play had yet to commence. Tugga just about chucked a mental when he walked in from the pitch inspection but as Punter explained, 'There's nothing wrong with a bit of rehearsal.'

The Poms resumed on 1 for 48 and despite the loss of Butcher for 41 they looked quite solid. I suggested to Tugga that he put a man at fine leg and, such is our captain's respect for my opinion, he immediately implemented a field change. I was moved to silly mid-on where I spent the next hour dodging balls. But fortunately the only serious injury occurred to Hussain, who was struck on the finger by one of Dizzy's high-speed thunderbolts. Hussain, or 'Poppadum' as he's known by certain sectors of the local press, immediately dropped his bat and fell to his knees in agony. Of course, no one likes to see a fellow

I was moved to silly mid-on where I spent the next hour dodging balls.

151

player injured and we all ran in to provide assistance, helping the distressed English skipper to his feet. Not that this was fully appreciated by some commentators who questioned my good sportsmanship at the time, claiming I 'mocked' the injured player. I thought he'd played a good innings and simply went to shake his hand — what's the problem with that? For us the removal of Hussain represented a vital piece of psychological damage and after he went no one put up any real resistance, the Poms collapsing to 9 for 164 before lunch and giving us victory by an innings and 118 runs. Appropriately enough Warney took the final wicket and in the chaos and euphoria of that moment we all rushed in to embrace, shake hands and try to grab a souvenir. In hindsight I now accept running off the field with Umpire Sharp's hat was a slight overstepping of the mark, but I was simply carried away by the moment.

We delayed our dressing-room celebrations to walk a lap of honour to acknowledge the large contingent of Aussies over here who really supported us. As a touring cricketer it means a lot just knowing that your countrymen have travelled halfway round the world to watch you play, and whenever we hear that cheer or feel a half-empty Foster's can land nearby, we know an Aussie is behind us. After thanking the crowd we headed for the rooms where a few of the England players dropped by for a drink and were promptly sprayed with one.

It's a tradition amongst the Aussie team that after a Test victory or one-day series win, everyone is cleared from the rooms while the players and officials gather to sing 'Under the Southern Cross', a song originally penned by Rod Marsh, although someone later cleaned it up a little and added the verbs. Today's rendition was one of the great experiences of my life. As Punter belted out the words each player hugged the bloke next to him. Even the fact that I ended up with my arm round a marketing rep from Bolle didn't detract from the moment — although our masseuse

In hindsight I accept that running off the field with Umpire Sharp's hat was a slight overstepping of the mark.

Rebecca Lauder almost did when she foolishly attempted to start harmonising. Fortunately she was ushered outside by team management. As was I an hour or so later for an interview with, I assumed, some local journo. Turned out to be a live television cross to Australia for an interview with The 7.30 Report's Kerry O'Brien. Months later I was shown a tape of this interview and, let's not make any bones about it, I was clearly pissed. Fortunately, so was he.

Mon July 9

I tell you what, there were a few bleary eyes this morning as we dragged ourselves out of bed to face a well-earned rest day. Down in the lobby I bumped into Greg 'Fat Cat' Ritchie who told me he is over here leading a supporters' tour. Apparently Fat Cat's the only one on this tour, but that hasn't stopped the big man enjoying his trip.

Tugga raised the possibility in the press this morning that if Australia wins the next Test then we should perhaps be allowed to take the original Ashes urn home with us, rather than just a replica as now occurs. However the Chief Executive of the England and Wales Cricket Board, Tim Lamb, has rejected the idea, saying the urn was too fragile to be transported. Same argument Christopher Skase used for years.

English captain Nasser Hussain got some bad news today from his specialist who told him he wouldn't be able to play for two weeks. He was naturally very disappointed as he was hoping for at least three or four. There's a bit of speculation about who will captain the Poms in the second Test, with Atherton, Stewart and Butcher all having tried and failed in the past. The only other options are Trescothick or placing an ad in the employment section of the *Times*. Apparently after the Test loss yesterday the Chairman of the England and Wales Cricket Board called a crisis meeting of the selectors for this Wednesday, but it has had to be postponed as they already had another crisis meeting scheduled for that night.

Most of the touring party and their wives/girlfriends headed off this morning in the hope of securing tickets for the Wimbledon final. We managed to get in and all decided to wear our baggy green caps, partly to show support for Pat Rafter, but mainly in the hope of free drinks. It was a great game, pity about the result.

Applicants for the job of England captain line up to be interviewed.

Tuesday July 10

I tell you what, the 7.30 am wake-up call came as a rude shock this morning. Honestly, I reckon I would have been lucky to have had two-hours sleep all night. Whether it was the air-conditioning, the noise or the fact we didn't get in 'til 5.30 am, I was feeling pretty average. With so many of the players having their kids staying at the team hotel, breakfasts have certainly become noisy, chaotic affairs — although since the kids arrived there have been fewer food fights taking place.

This morning I sat across from Pigeon's young son who has just started eating solids, mainly bread and mushed up corn flakes. This kid now boasts a diet more varied than Warney's.

Wherever we Aussies go, there always seems to be a fair contingent of journos following our every move and this morning I happened to bump into a columnist from the *Daily Telegraph* by the name of Geoffrey Haines who had recently written an article questioning my place in the one-day squad. Now normally I don't even read the crap that's written about me but this piece really pissed me off and I took the opportunity of telling the bloke so. Confronting a journalist can be a hazardous exercise. Generally there can only be one winner and that's the person with the pen in

Golf is a great game and can be enjoyed by both the fellas . . .

their hand. But on this occasion I had a bat in my hand and I think the smarmy little shit might at the very least be retracting the claim that 'Warwick Todd lacks aggression'.

It's often difficult to find an activity on tour the wives and girlfriends can enjoy along with the fellas but today we solved the problem. We played golf and allowed the girls to caddy.

. . . and the ladies.

Wednesday July 11

An early start this morning saw the boys bidding farewell to their partners and climbing onto the bus for the trip west to Taunton. Australian Cricket Board rules are quite clear on the point that during the Test matches wives and girlfriends can stay with the players, but during county fixtures the team must exist without family. Some trendy, leftie types have seen this as 'sexist' but in truth it simply gives us boys a chance to bond as a unit without the whingeing, divisive, petty interference you so often get from women. What's sexist about that?

For decades the Aussie team has stayed at Taunton's Castle Hotel but this time we've moved to the rival Posthouse Hotel which has a better gym and a pool. They also offered drink cards to all senior players which helped clinch the deal.

According to the papers, England is no closer to settling on a stand-in captain. Gough apparently put his hand up yesterday but unfortunately strained a finger doing so and may miss a week. Meanwhile Butcher, Atherton and Stewart have all pretty much indicated they don't want the job which is quite amazing when you consider that any Australian player would kill to be captain.

Speaking of captains, Punter will get his chance to lead the side this week after it was decided that Tugga, Pigeon and Warney would all have some time off to spend with their families. Gilly will stay on as 12th man just to 'keep an eye on things', but team management seem to have a lot of confidence in Punter's ability to handle the reins, and right from the start he's taken his leadership role seriously. Upon arriving at the hotel he called a quick team meeting saying, 'If anyone has any problems my door is always open. I won't be in but help yourselves to the mini-bar.' He then cancelled training and shot out the door.

With no practice to worry about the boys went their own ways this afternoon. Flemo, Dizzy and Secco enjoyed a few hours of ten-pin bowling while Funky had his hair dyed red for the clash against Sommerset this Friday. Meanwhile Junior, Slats and Punter visited a tattoo parlour in downtown Taunton to have an emblem of the Southern Cross applied to their ankles. It was a wonderful gesture and a typical instance of team bonding.

Gough receives the news he won't be required to captain England.

Thursday July 12

Slats, Junior and Punter are all doubtful for tomorrow's match having been diagnosed with a freak bout of blood poisoning. Adding to our injury woes, Binger has a soreness at the base of his ribs that Hooter feels might cause a few problems, so Pigeon and Warney drove down this morning to be here on stand-by if needed. The only hitch is that the hotel is fully booked and a couple of blokes may now have to share rooms. I tell you what, it's not easy putting up with someone else in your 'space' after so many months of living solo and we're all hoping we don't draw the short straw. Of course a few years back it was standard for Aussie cricketers to share rooms and you could really be stuck with some pretty ordinary co-tenants. I remember on a tour of the West Indies once hearing a certain opening batsman complain at breakfast about his room-mate's habit of relieving himself in the shower. 'What's wrong with having a pee in the shower?' someone asked, to which the batsman replied, 'Who said anything about having a pee?' You get the general idea.

Training today was at the hotel gym and then the ground. Being a county match Somerset are likely to follow England's traditional policy of fielding a substandard team for the game, a policy the Poms now appear to be extending to Test matches. According to the papers, Atherton has finally agreed to stand in as captain for the second Test at Lords, having been threatened by team management that if he refused they'd appoint him as a selector.

Running through a few stretches and warm-up exercises.

It was decided to hold separate batting and bowling meetings tonight where the two groups of players could really focus on the issues specific to them. But due to a slight mix-up we both ended up in the same beer garden. Back at the hotel there was good news for me on the room-sharing front with our reserves agreeing to bunk in together. Just as well really, given my room has only one double bed and a single, a combination always guaranteed to cause arguments between room-mates. Back in the old days of sharing rooms there used to be various methods of deciding who would get the double bed: blokes from Western Australia and Queensland would toss a coin, Victorians and New South Welshmen would go on seniority, while of course the South Australians would just hop in together.

Friday July 13

Australia vs Somerset
County Ground, Day 1

At 7.15 this morning a bunch of bleary-eyed Aussie cricketers climbed onto the bus for the short trip to the county ground. It wasn't until 9.40 when we crossed the Welsh border that we realised it was the wrong bus.

At the team meeting last night it had been decided that in view of Binger's rib injury we would rest him and play Noffke today. For the young medium pacer it was a dream come true, soured only by the shocking haircut Bing had inflicted on his replacement overnight with the dreaded number-one blades. It was supposed to be a 'trim' but went horribly wrong and Noffke was heard protesting, 'I can't go onto the field like this, I look ridiculous!' Mind you, it's a situation that never stopped Greg Matthews. In the end our debutant bowler was forced to wear a training cap to hide his unfortunate hairstyle.

Our new captain Punter won the toss and, out of reflex action, immediately offered opposing captain Michael Burns 'double or nothing'. We ended up batting. As has come to be expected Somerset decided to rest several of their regular line-up for this match but did enlist the services of Pakistani stars Shoaib Akhtar and Aamir Sohall, giving them a pretty full-strength side. We on the other hand elected to field just three batsman, six bowlers and a room attendant.

Akhtar opened with a fiery spell, hitting Slats on several occasions and forcing Hados to take evasive action, which he did very effectively by getting out for just 6 and spending the rest of the day sheltering in the dressing-room. But Punter wasn't to be intimidated, smashing a magnificent 128 off just 130 balls. I was robbed of any decent time at the crease by one of the worst umpiring decisions of my Test career. On just 11, I was given out caught behind, but didn't actually get near the ball. In fact, it must have missed my bat by two inches — a point I was trying to demonstrate to the umpire when he cited me for making an offensive gesture, at which point I did actually make one. Not a good day.

I simply indicated to the umpire that the ball had missed my bat by two inches.

Saturday July 14

Australia vs Somerset
County Ground, Day 2

With rain yet again delaying the start of play this morning, we decided to declare our innings on the overnight score of 348 and use the opportunity to watch the third and deciding rugby Test between the Wallabies and the Lions. The timely downpour allowed us to take over the Taunton committee room where we screamed and barracked for the boys back home, baring our arses at the screen every time the Lions got anywhere near the ball and spraying Foster's in the air as the Aussies made up vital ground. It was a great way to pass the morning and I just hope the ladies from the Taunton Quilt Society who were holding their AGM at the time weren't too greatly inconvenienced.

When play finally got under way we soon had Somerset in all sorts of trouble thanks largely to a blistering spell from Flem who picked up 6 for 59. Dizzy also bowled well, regularly clocking over 140 km/h. And that was off the short run-up. All in all it was a good day in the field, marred only by some of the crowd's unsportsmanlike behaviour. At a lot of these county games the grounds are quite small and comments of a vocal (and often drunk) minority can be heard quite clearly. If these comments are of a humorous or light-hearted nature no one really minds but today a group of spectators really got stuck into me on quite a personal level. I won't repeat any of the language, needless to say it was quite offensive and f*#k me if it didn't keep up all day. Every time I went to field anywhere near this section of the ground these bozos would start heckling. It was only after getting back to the rooms that I realised what Katto had written on the back of my shirt.

It was only later that I realised what Katto had written on the back of my shirt.

Sunday July 15

Australia vs Somerset, County Ground, Day 3

In hindsight, last night's go-karting team challenge may have been a mistake.

Having made it through much of this tour without any real injury worries we've now hit quite a few all at once. Slats has a badly bruised wrist, Hados's knee is giving him trouble, Binger is still battling a rib strain and I've got a very stiff neck. I guess in hindsight last night's go-kart team challenge may have been a mistake, but at least it got us out of the hotel.

With Somerset all out for 267 at the end of play yesterday we decided to mix up the batting order so everyone could have a little time in the middle. Unfortunately no one explained this theory to Marto who proceeded to hog the bowling all day with a selfish and, if I do say so myself, grandstanding 176 not out. It was practically 3.00 in the afternoon and I'd barely finished digesting the apple upside-down cake we had for lunch when I finally got the chance to pad up. As it turned out I only got to face a couple of local bowlers as by this stage Somerset's highly paid paceman Shoaib Akhtar had left the field with 'cramp in both legs'. It can't have been that severe as he could be seen quite clearly during the afternoon session chatting to some blonde on the player's balcony. But Akhtar or no Akhtar, I was desperate for some solid batting practice prior to the next Test, so you can imagine my dismay when Marto and I looked up to see our skipper waving us in from the rooms — a surprise declaration on just 335. It later turned out Punter hadn't meant for us to come in. He was just waving to Akhtar's girlfriend up on the balcony, but by this stage it was too late to reverse the decision. At the end of the day Somerset were 1 for 52 chasing a total of 416 for victory.

Monday July 16

Australia vs Somerset, County Ground, Day 4

As the empty grandstands suggested, today was never going to be a high point of county cricket. A lacklustre display saw the home team all out for 240, giving us victory by 177 runs. On the positive side, our injury list seems to be shortening, with Hados and Slats both confident of being fit for the next Test. Meanwhile Binger was given an extensive net session this afternoon, bowling full speed to Buck and showing no signs of discomfort. As opposed to our coach who looked so uncomfortable he just about shat himself.

The early finish gave me an opportunity to catch up with a few sponsors over here in England, a job all professional cricketers must take time out to do if they hope to secure lucrative contracts. Some sponsorship arrangements can be quite 'high maintenance', like my footwear suppliers, Reebok, who demand photo shoots, in-store appearances and constant promotional work. Last year in Australia I even had to pull on the Santa suit and host their bloody Christmas party. But hopefully after that incident with the corporate affairs manager's daughter who, incidentally, insisted on sitting on my lap, I won't be asked again. Other sponsors are of course a lot less demanding, like Qantas with whom I have a unique deal. They offer me free business-class travel anywhere in the world on only one condition — that I do it with Ansett.

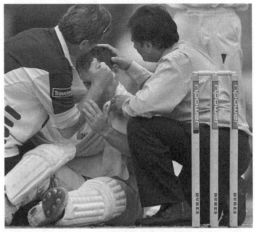

Binger showed no signs of discomfort bowling in the nets — unlike those he was bowling to.

Tuesday July 17

England's fitness advisor sends one down.

After a big night on the town celebrating our win at a local nightclub I was looking forward to a decent sleep-in but it was not to be. A phone call came through at 7.15 from a taxi driver saying I'd left something in his cab, which I thought was pretty good of him. Until he insisted I come round and help clean it up, at which point I denied all knowledge of the trip and referred him to our media manager.

A brief workout session this morning cleared all players fit for selection with our only injury worry now Funky's hair. The pink he chose for the match against Somerset is a shocker and he's been desperately attempting to bleach it out, but has only succeeded in giving himself a patch of blonde at the back.

As usual there was a throng of media types and hangers-on back at the hotel for a press conference and the questions to Tugga flew thick and fast:

'Will there be any changes from the last Test match?' (*Daily Mirror*)
'What's the feeling like in the camp?' (*Telegraph*)
'Will Justin Langer play?' (Justin Langer)

Traditionally the ACB pays for the pre-Test players' dinner and the boys always enjoy choosing an eating establishment likely to rack up a decent bill. We certainly managed that tonight, setting what I believe to be a team record. The restaurant itself wasn't all that expensive, it was more the fact that it was in Paris. Special guest speaker for our dinner was South African rugby union captain Francois Pinear who spoke about how tough it was in the early days of his career. Even at the height, he told us that he was forced to work as a nightclub bouncer just to make ends meet. It was an inspirational speech (perhaps a little on the gloomy side) and certainly confirmed what I've long believed — that when it comes to sport, kids these days have it far too easy. They're straight out of school, off to the

Training underway at England's newly completed cricket academy.

cricket academy, they practically have a sunglasses and footwear sponsorship deal handed to them on a plate, and then it's into the team with lots of cosy meetings and confidence-building exercises. When I first joined the Australian team in '86 the then captain Allan Border didn't say a word to me for the first five years. During that time we roomed together, played 43 Tests — I was even best man at his wedding. That's what it's all about.

Speaking of ex-captains, coming back from dinner I bumped into Ritchie Benaud at the airport. Unfortunately we didn't get much of a chance to chat as he was walking in one direction and the policeman I was handcuffed to was walking in the other.

Wednesday July 18

After our final training session this morning the team for tomorrow was announced with Binger given the nod over Flem as third bowler. Tugga later confided to me that he actually preferred Flem but was simply too scared to tell Bing he'd been dropped.

Also on the agenda for this morning was the taking of our official Ashes squad photo, an event always plagued by problems and disputes. First we have to sort out the seating in precise order of seniority, then sit around waiting for the light to improve, then there's always someone who blinks just at the wrong moment or who felt they were masked by someone else. As it turned out though, this morning's shoot went remarkably smoothly and team management seemed very happy with the final shot taken. I'd hate to be around when the film gets processed and they discover a certain middle-order batsman had his old fella hanging out.

Hados's ears weren't the only things pulled out during our team photo.

Training turned ugly today after an *alleged* high tackle on Punter brought the big man down.

At the team meeting we spent a great deal of time scrutinising the England top five batsmen. The reason it took so long was that we couldn't name that many. So we concentrated on their top three and formulated a mini-plan for each focusing on their perceived weaknesses, whether technical or personal. For example, Thorpe: hasn't played for six weeks, has tendency to shuffle across crease leaving leg stump exposed, hates eggplant. Precisely how this last piece of information could be turned to our advantage on the field remains unclear, but at the international level everything counts. Another player we focused on was stand-in captain Michael Atherton. Once again we formed a profile: he's struggling with form, swore he'd never be captain again, and hates being called 'Mike' or 'Mikey'. On top of this it was at Lords in '94 that Mikey was caught pulling dirt from his pocket and applying it to the ball, an act of blatant ball tampering we shall be sure to remind him of when he arrives at the crease. All in all it was a good meeting and after it finished we all headed back to our rooms to prepare for the big match tomorrow and to work on our poems. Our expectations of a win at Lords are high but we're being careful not to get too far ahead of ourselves. Overconfidence is the biggest danger we face but I'm sure it won't be a problem for us.

Thursday July 19

Australia vs England
2nd Test, Lords, Day 1

We've come this far but our job is not done
Until we can say the Ashes we've won.
This is the second Test and Lords is the venue,
Let's hope we can win and that smoked salmon's on the menu.

(Adam Gilchrist, read before play, Day 1)

Lords. No matter how many times you play at this great ground it's still a thrill just to arrive and soak in the atmosphere. There's so much history everywhere you look. Old Father Time above the Tavern Stand and of course the players' balcony, which has been the stage for so many celebratory moments from us Aussies in recent years that it has now been fitted with a non-slip surface, safety rails and a smoker's

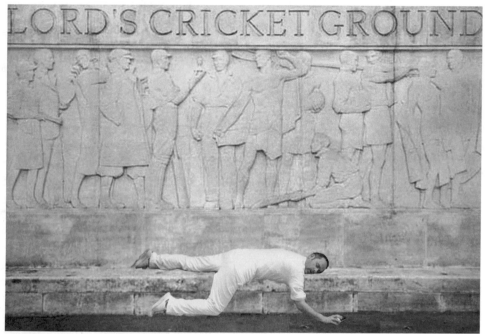

I like getting to the ground early. In this case, I was still there from the night before.

trough. There's also a special feeling when you walk into the rooms here and see the honour boards listing everyone who has ever scored a 'five for', a century or a $2000 match fine.

Tugga won the toss and elected to send the Poms in but play was delayed by poor weather. We spent the hour and a half rain delay kicking a footy in the outfield and having slips practice before the first overs were finally bowled by Pigeon and Dizzy. Even then the light was pretty poor, a fact clearly illustrated when Junior, the safest pair of hands in slips, completely missed a catch off Atherton. In fact, he didn't even see the ball until it had flown past. Although whether the light was totally to blame remains unclear as a little later in the day Umpire Holder tossed Junior his jumper and he completely missed that too. Trescothick was the first wicket to fall, caught behind off Dizzy, but we were unable to capitalise on the moment as once again rain forced everyone from the ground.

A highlight of the Lords Test is getting to meet the Queen and during the luncheon interval we were instructed by team management on how to conduct ourselves. There would be no asking for autographs (as Merv once did!), no chewing gum, Hados was to be fully clothed at all times and no smoking until the royal entourage had left the Long Room. When we finally assembled at tea for the official occasion, Tugga was looking nervous as he had the job of introducing each member of the team to Her Majesty, a task he stuffed up during the World Cup in '99 when he completely forgot Flem's name. Today he got through all of our names without a problem, but then somehow managed to forget hers, which can easily happen when you're under pressure. Speaking of the '99 World Cup, I remember the royal reception back then when all players were asked to line up in their respective teams to meet the Queen and Prince Phillip. Murray Goodwin from Zimbabwe somehow found himself standing with the Windies team and caused a minor stir when being introduced to Prince Philip, who apparently said 'You don't look too much like a West Indian.' To which Murray replied, 'No, but I wish I was hung like one.' Fortunately the joke went down well and His Royal Highness replied, 'Yes, those niggers do have big dicks don't they', before being ushered away by a royal protocol officer whose full-time job is standing by for just such comments. Luckily today was not marked by any such controversy. The Queen simply moved along the line, exchanging handshakes and pleasantries (and, in the case of Warney, a phone number) before heading back to the palace.

We in turn headed back onto the field where three quick wickets in the final session saw England struggle to 4 for 121. Perhaps the most satisfying of these was Atherton, lbw to his old foe Pigeon. The acting England captain had been looking in good touch and was on 37 when he failed to offer a shot. Naturally we were all pretty pumped to see him go and ran in for our customary celebrations, hugging and patting each other on the back. I admit in hindsight that attempting a high five with umpire Steve Bucknor may have been a slight overstepping of the line, but we were carried away by the moment. It was tight, pressure-packed cricket and each Pommy batsman was greeted with a few well-chosen pleasantries as they arrived at or departed the crease. Predictably the 'experts' up in the commentary box made much of our 'sustained sledging' but it wasn't really that bad. In fact, the most heated exchange I heard all day took place between Dizzy and Bing over who should get first use of the new ball.

Friday July 20

Australia vs England
2nd Test, Lords, Day 2

Take my hand, we're halfway there,
Whoooooah, we're living on a prayer.

(Michael Slater, sung badly before play, Day 2)

When we arrived at the ground this morning the super-sopa was hard at work trying to mop up the Australian dressing-room after last night's post-match drinks session. Why they carpet this place is anyone's guess. Another sell-out crowd of 30000 saw England dismissed right on lunch, thanks to a brilliant bowling spell from Pigeon (5 for 54), backed up by relentlessly brilliant catching from the rest of us. This fact is often overlooked by certain fast bowlers who seem to think that they are single-handedly responsible for taking wickets. Our sharpness in the field was perhaps typified by a blinder of a catch Punter took off Cork, diving across in front of Junior and coming up with the prized red cherry. Everyone immediately dashed in to con-gratulate him on the effort, except for Junior who just stood there at second slip saying 'It was my f*#king catch.' To his credit, Cork actually made 24 runs and took on some pretty fierce bowling from Pigeon, hitting our strike bowler to the boundary on several occasions. Most quicks are fairly predictable and after being hit for 4 they will invari-ably follow up with a bumper, but Pigeon is a real thinker. He totally took Cork by surprise by following up with 7 bumpers and a stream of abuse.

Even though the Pom's first innings total of 121 was not all that daunting we got off to a bad start with Hados out for a duck. Our new Number 3, Punter, then strode to the crease obviously determined to play his natural game, which he did, being dismissed for just 14. At 2 for 27 things were looking a little dire but Junior and Slats then set about steadying the ship. At the tea break Junior was on 93 not out and clearly very nervous about the prospect of his first

I'm all for grabbing a few souvenirs, but if you ask me Junior's just being greedy.

Test century at Lords. We could tell he was trying not to think about the time eight years ago when he got out on 99 to Phil Tufnell — not easy as we were all reminding him of it. But Junior kept his nerve and soon after notched up a fine century. He was run out shortly after, an event that saw Warwick Todd leave the Lords dressing-room for that long, familiar walk.

Once I got back from the dunny it was time to head out onto the playing arena. It's a journey familiar to all Test players: out the back door of the change-rooms, down two flights of stairs, into the esteemed Long Room, past Jeff Thompson at the bar and through a bunch of ancient MCC members all calling out the same ancient witticisms, 'See you in a minute!' or 'Good luck, but not too much!' Naturally you take such comments in good humour and I was later shocked to be informed that I'd been accused of 'jostling' a member. If anything this bloke went at me, quite aggressively in fact. I simply asked him to move, he stood his ground and we lightly made contact. To suggest, as several papers did, that I would deliberately 'head-butt a 93-year-old club member' is simply outrageous and I'll be demanding a retraction from the journalists involved.

With only a few overs remaining before stumps I was determined not to play any rash shots, preferring to leave that to Gilly while I concentrated on simple survival. The Poms were bowling quite viciously with a lot of short stuff and I was hit on several occasions. But we held out and made it to 5 for 255 at the close of play.

Naturally there were a few drinks back in the rooms to celebrate Junior's first century at Lords and Pigeon's big 5-wicket haul and I took the opportunity of making sure their names were added to the Lords honour boards that hang on the dressing-room walls.

Tugga congratulates Junior on a fine century. This is believed to be the only photo in existence of the two brothers making actual physical contact.

Saturday July 21

Australia vs England
2nd Test, Lords, Day 3

This is the time, we know what to do,
Get out there and fight, see this game through,
It's up to me and it's up to you,
Let's make it happen here on Day 2.

(Glenn McGrath, read before play, Day 3)

The last thing you want on the morning of a Test is to be woken by a phone call at 7.05 am, especially when that call is from the Secretary of the Marylebone Cricket Club demanding the Lords honour boards be returned immediately. Frankly I can't even remember ripping them off the wall but then again I can't remember anything after about 6.30 last night.

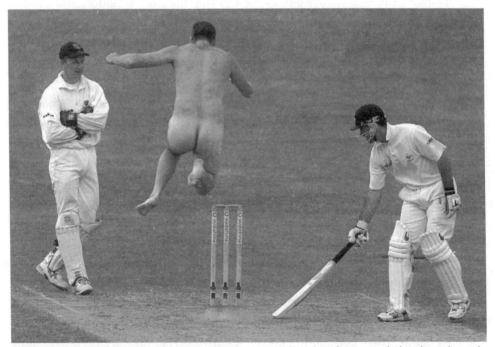

There's no doubting England's coach Duncan Fletcher was under a lot of pressure during the series and in the end he must have simply cracked.

The ball was clearly going to miss leg-stump. Unfortunately it hit middle stump.

There was great excitement on the way to the ground this morning when the team bus passed Elle McPherson filming a movie here in London. Naturally there was lots of banging on the windows and the odd bare-arsed salute as we drove past a fellow Aussie making a name for herself on the international stage. Hopefully that's what we'll be able to do at Lords today as we edge closer to a record 7th straight Ashes series win.

I resumed my place at the crease with Gilly only to see the Australian vice-captain dropped by Butcher off the very first ball of the day. This moment was to pretty much sum up England's fielding for the match and Gilly was actually dropped four times. Finally, on 90 he was caught behind off Gough by Stewart, who immediately threw the ball into the air in delight, and then dropped it. As usual I was happy to play the anchoring role, picking off the singles and rotating the strike while Gilly played his natural, flashy brand of selfish, look-at-me cricket. When he was dismissed the English bowlers seemed to step up a gear, Gough and Cork in particular sending down a torrid spell of short-pitched bowling. Warney had barely just arrived at the crease when he failed to evade a bruising delivery from Gough which took him right on the upper leg. As fate would have it he wasn't wearing a thigh pad but fortunately the ball hit a nicotine patch that slightly dulled the impact. On 37 I left a ball from Caddick that, in my opinion, was clearly going to miss off-stump. An opinion that was proved correct when the ball slammed into my middle stump and I was forced to make the long walk back up the stairs and through the Long Room, which had been evacuated at the fall of my wicket. We ended up with a final total of 401, a lead of 214.

Tugga didn't need to say much in the rooms between innings. Looking round I think we all knew we were on the verge of victory and it was just a question of crushing the Poms, coming out hard and driving their defeated carcass into the dust. Then we could all get together and share a drink.

Trescothick fell first, followed by the prized scalp of Atherton, but it was the wicket of Thorpe that probably did the most damage. He was hit on the hand by Bing, who proceeded to bowl him just a few balls later. It was a terrifyingly fast spell from the New South Wales paceman, who was clearly back to his fiery best, with quite a few deliveries actually landing on the pitch. Every ball was accompanied by a stream of verbal abuse that some commentators described as 'ugly and unsettling'. All I can say is you should have seen him during the team darts night in Taunton last week. At stumps England were in a spot of bother at 4 for 163, still 51 runs behind. To make matters worse, their star batsman Graham Thorpe had to be taken to hospital for x-rays on a suspected broken hand. He was cleared of a fracture but eye-witnesses claim he could later be seen outside the hospital jamming his hand into a car door in the hope of being overlooked for the third Test.

Bing's behaviour was described as 'angry and unsettling'. You should have seen him during the team darts competition last week.

Sunday July 22

Australia vs England
2nd Test, Lords, Day 4

We've climbed the hill boys, we're now on the ridge,
Let's make sure we've got enough beer in the fridge.

(*Warwick Todd, read before play, Day 4*)

Well it didn't take long for the old firm of Pigeon and Dizzy to clean up the Pommy tail — England all out for 227. And with just 14 runs required for victory, all was in readiness for a few post-match celebrations in our dressing-room with the fridge stocked, carpet rolled back and residents within half a kilometre warned to stay indoors. Of course, chasing a small target is never easy and our openers were reminded by Tugga of the need to get out there and play it safe. Slats understood perfectly and held himself back right throughout the first over, after which he

inexplicably charged Caddick and was caught at second slip for just 4. Punter also fell to the third ball he faced, but despite these setbacks the total was soon reached by Hados and Junior, giving us victory with 8 wickets to spare.

After the presentation ceremony it was time for lunch and with so many of the guys having their wives and kids at the ground, our celebrations became quite a family affair. We kicked off with the whole team having lunch in the players' dining room. Then, while the womenfolk got on with the dishes, we boys headed to our dressing-rooms for some serious partying. It's not the first time wives and girlfriends have been involved with our post-match festivities. Here at Lords after the '99 World Cup final win we felt that they'd been such a huge part of our success that we decided

Grounds staff search the Lords pitch for bone fragments from Graham Thorpe's hand.

to even let them into the pavilion, provided they didn't stay too long or attempt to take part in the singing.

There's nothing quite like the feeling of a Test win at Lords and with Slats acting as DJ the place was soon rocking. Finally around 8.00 pm it was time for the special moment sacred to all Aussie players: the singing of the team song. Everyone gathered round Punter who stood astride the physio's bench ready to lead the chorus. Warney held aloft a mobile phone so that, we assumed, the injured Nathan Bracken back in Australia could be part of the moment. It later turned out he just had some nurse from Derbyshire on the other end, but in the excitement no one really cared. I tell you what, being there in the rooms listening to 'Under the Southern Cross', it's a moment when you wish time would stand still. And that Punter would learn to sing. It certainly was a night to remember. Just a pity none of us can.

Monday July 23

I have no recollection of this day. Possibly returned to hotel.

Tuesday July 24

Still pretty hazy. I remember being asked for my signature and to pose for some photographs by some very persistent English fans, which was okay, but when they started demanding fingerprints I realised something was wrong. Then blacked out again.

Wednesday July 25

Good news, the charges have all been dropped. Seems that as they can't prove exactly which one of us it was who urinated from the top of London's Millennium Wheel, the prosecution will not proceed.

Praise for our crushing second Test win has been high with many journos once again comparing us to the 1948 Invincibles. As always though there have been the knockers, including one 'expert' from the *Daily Mirror* who has actually questioned my place in the team for the next Test, suggesting I was playing poorly and that many younger members of the squad deserved a place ahead of me! Normally I'd laugh off something like this (after referring it to my lawyers for possible defamation proceedings), but the fact is there's been a bit of criticism recently about my form and questions concerning my long-term future. An article just a few days back quoted a 'source close to the team' — which had to be Katto or Marto — saying I was bringing down team morale by constantly being seen on the physio's table. This is a claim I find outrageous given that the only reason I'm on the table is to enable me to get back out there on the paddock, and the fact that a lot of my injuries happen to have been golf-related is simply not relevant. Still, I couldn't argue with the claim that my form so far on tour has been a little patchy and the selectors certainly showed with Lang that they weren't afraid of making changes to the team, even if it meant a long-standing member missed out.

Rather than sit around stewing over the situation, I decided to confront it head on and so after breakfast I dropped by Tugga's room for a chat. Basically I put my place in the team on the line saying, 'If there is someone you, as a selector, think would be better I'm happy to step aside.' Naturally I didn't mean a word of it but to my horror he seemed to take this offer quite seriously. Told me he'd actually been thinking about introducing a bit of youth into the side and agreed that perhaps it was time for me to step aside. I gotta tell you, it wasn't exactly what I wanted to hear. There's a difference between straight shooting and a bullet through the head. In the end we both agreed to have a think about the situation and I left in a bit of a daze.

Was it time for Warwick Todd to hang up the boots? A thousand thoughts went through my head. I mean, cricket's been my life for the best part of sixteen years (seventeen if you count the season with Tasmania). In that time it has brought me so much. I own a beautiful home and wife, head my own charitable foundation, I've travelled the world, sat on boards of inquiry (or at least appeared before them), and dined with everyone from heads of state to show-business superstars. Was I really ready to give all that away? But what if I tried to stay on and ended up being dropped for the third Test? I'd lose a lot of self-esteem, not to mention a whole range of clothing and footwear sponsorships from companies not keen to be associated with a loser. I think I wandered around London for most of the afternoon trying to sort things out in my head. I even rang Ros back home and it was great hearing her comforting voice and that reassuring perspective on the situation, 'Hi, I'm not in right now but leave a message after the beep.' In the end I decided the best thing would be to sleep on the problem and make a decision in the morning.

Todd dumped!

Troubled Test star dropped from Aussie team

By **CHRIS JEFFRIES**

Despite their crushing win in the recent Lords Test, Australian selectors have dumped long-serving batsman Warwick Todd for the upcoming match at Trent Bridge. Team manager Steve Bernard confirmed today that the controversial left-hander had been omitted from the line-up after a string of low scores and off-field controversies, the most recent of which involved a drunken romp on the upper deck of a London bus. Sources close to the team have confirmed that Todd's place in the team has been under scrutiny for quite some time. No replacement has yet been named.

Meanwhile England coach Duncan Fletcher has defended his team's recent performances, telling reporters, "We musn't show panic, alarm or despondency." Fletcher made the comments before attempting to jump from a fourteenth-storey window ledge outside his Kensington home.

Warwick Todd is
proud to be associated with the
following fine companies:

HIH Insurance

One.Tel

Ansett

Thankyou list

David Mitchiner   Local photographer
Deb Brash   Design and production
Robert Taylor   Photo manipulations
Jack Atley   Test photographs
Jenny Mills   Photo research

Special thanks to

Debra Choate; Nikki Hamilton; Pauline Hirsh; Carly Lord;
Susannah Mott; Vanitha Naidu; Jacqui Wells

Thanks also to

Damien Booth; Todd Emery; Shaun Graf; Adam Lange;
Clayton Lasscock; Javier Markham; Rick Olarenshaw;
Martine Pearman; Billy Pinnell; Sharron Singer; Joshua Singer.

Victorian Cricket Association; Greyhound Pioneer Australia;
Carlton & United Breweries; The Hotel Como, Melbourne

Photo sources

All photos by David Mitchiner except:

AP/AAP Image 80, Colour 9 (bottom)

Jack Atley   10, 55, 59, 93, 101, 120, 128, ,131, 134, 136, 138, 140, 145, 146, 148, 151, 152, 154, 155, 156, 161, 162, 163, 164, 170, Colour 5 (bottom), 7, 9, 15, 16.

Getty Images   Allsport 15, 29, 42, 48, 59, 68, 71, 97(left), 106, 108(top), 108 (centre), 147, Colour 3 (top right), 4 (top), 5 (top left), 6, 7 (top), 14 (top); Image Bank 6.

Newsphotos   *Courier Mail* 150; *Daily Telegraph* 74, 164 (top); *Herald-Sun* 4 (bottom left), 19, 32, 83, 109, 124, 130, 143, 160, 173, Colour 1 (top), 4, 13; *Sunday-Age* 171; *Sunday Herald-Sun* 124; *Sunday Mail* 120; The *Australian* 61, 169, 174, Colour 2 (top).

Mark Ray   153

Reuters   57, 132

We apologise if there are any omissions.

Todd drives straight into trouble

Test cricketer Warwick Todd was yesterday fined $200 in the Brisbane Magistrate's Court for illegally leaving his car in a disabled parking space while on the way to a testimonial luncheon. Magistrate John Denham rejected Todd's argument that as he was "pretty pissed at the time" this constituted a disability. Todd was fined $40 for the parking offence and a further $200 for the admission that he was inebriated.